Jane McLoughlin was born in Kent. She was educated at several English schools, and Trinity College, Dublin. She has worked as a tractor driver, civil service clerk, bookshop manager, university research assistant, hotel factotum and flower-picker.

As a journalist, she worked on the staff of the *Daily Mirror*, *Daily Telegraph*, *Daily Mail* and *Observer*. She was Business Editor and Women's Editor of the *Guardian*. She has contributed to the *Financial Times*, *Evening Standard* City Pages, the *Farmers' Weekly*, *New Statesman*, and the *International Herald Tribune*.

Her books include *The Demographic Revolution* (Faber 1991); *The Everywoman Guide to Women and Employment* (Unwin Hyman 1989), and, as a co-author, *Asia's New Industrial World* (Methuen 1985).

Her first novel, *Coincidence*, will be published by Virago in 1992.

JANE McLOUGHLIN

Up and Running

WOMEN IN BUSINESS

Published by VIRAGO PRESS Limited 1992
20–23 Mandela Street
Camden Town
London NW1 0HQ

Jane McLoughlin © 1992

A CIP catalogue record for this book is available from the British Library

Printed in Great Britain by
Cox & Wyman Ltd, Reading, Berkshire

ACKNOWLEDGEMENTS

There is no adequate way for me to thank the numbers of busy and high-powered women who were prepared to give me their time and trust to make it possible to write this book. To maintain their anonymity, I cannot even list their names. But they know who they are, and each one has my sincere gratitude and thanks. They were unfailingly generous and stimulating, with the added bonus that in every case, I really enjoyed interviewing them. Never, even at the far end of several hours of tape, did the interest of what they had to say begin to flag.

My grateful thanks, too, to Treasury Minister Gillian Shephard, and to Lynda Gratton, of the London Business School, for their willing help; to Gillian Beaumont for her excellent copy-editing; and to Lennie Goodings of Virago, for her invaluable enthusiasm and support – *sine qua non*!

CONTENTS

PREFACE

This book is about all the women who believe that living happily ever after is a personal challenge to achieve. (Theirs are no fairy stories, and the book is *for* all the women who want to believe that their wishes can come true . . .)

Over the last twentysomething years, a few key women have been rewriting history. This book explores what that means to individual women, and to society's entire perception of womanhood.

We are all aware that this has changed, of course. But most examination of the how and why – and who – of change is still set firmly in the concrete overcoat of the way we were. There are many excellent books about women and careers, but they tend to see women in terms of an assumption of weakness – either as 'How To Overcome F As In Failure', or 'How To Blend Business and Babies'. What I wanted to do in this book was to demonstrate how the context of women's lives has moved beyond this, and been utterly changed through work: and, by letting the women at the forefront of that change talk about who and what they are, reach some understanding of what womanhood has come to mean to businesswomen today.

It sounded a tall order, certainly, but I became increasingly enthralled as the picture unfolded. What was most exciting about talking to these women – from successful business pioneers in their forties and fifties, who started out in the face of corporate consensus that women's place was in the home, to high-flying executives in their twenties who take equal opportunity as read – was a real sense of women getting somewhere.

Twenty years ago, any aspiring young woman knew that a

potential employer's reaction to her application for a job hinged on the assumption that she would marry, have children, and drop off the hierarchical ladder. He thought even training her was a waste of time and money because, unlike the boys, her Career would not be her Life. Today, some large corporate employers actually *prefer* women.

In the process, of course, we have changed. The Pill and equal education opportunities and the Women's Movement have all expanded our perception of what is possible for ourselves and each other. This certainly does not mean that misogyny has been banished from our society, but as independent people, we now have a range of options we did not have before.

Even so, I feel that a lot of us are not always aware of the choices we do have. Some will say that the women I have interviewed, who demonstrate how the perception of womanhood has changed, are not representative of most women – because these women are all ambitious and successful in business, far removed from the low-paid, part-time woman in a mundane job, the 'average' who makes up most of the eleven million women who constitute 47 per cent of the workforce in this country.

Yet fifteen years ago, when nine million women worked, the proportion of those who were successful businesswomen was much, much smaller – not even a full one per cent, whereas they are now 6 per cent of working women. I would argue that that tiny proportion in the early days played the major part in shifting the corporate ground and swinging the workplace culture in women's favour.

This is why this book concentrates on women in business – whether they are corporate executives or running their own operation outside the established hierarchical office system. All control large budgets; all have power of hire and fire, and therefore control the lives of other people, many of them men.

You may ask, 'why business, rather than the professions or civil servants or politicians?' In the mid 1980s, I worked as first Business Editor and then Women's Editor of the *Guardian*. It was in the business world that I sensed a cultural shift in favour of women. This came in the 'new' financial and technological industries which had no track record of male chauvinism. Then, after the manufacturing bloodletting of the early 1980s, business itself was in a state of flux, and this, too, made it a testing ground for gauging the growing 'feminisation' of the work culture.

That word feminisation, however hideous, is an illustration of the linguistic problems posed by the process of change. The language of business reflects the developing gender balance in a hitherto male-dominated culture. But as it moves away from an established masculine vocabulary, it has been forced to draw on the neutered jargon of technology to avoid overtones of sexuality. It is ironic how often key words used to communicate a greater degree of humanity in the workplace have to be borrowed from mechanical electronics.

Business is also an open-entry arena in the sense that women precluded from the professions by lack of academic qualifications or technical experience have been able to go it alone, starting their own businesses, and making a success of them. And, not so very incidentally, the skills involved in Bringing Up A Family are uniquely recognised here as relevant experience, rather than 'time out'.

The women I talked to are a small sample in statistical terms. I make no excuse for arguing from the particular to the general. Twenty years ago, we all suffered quite enough because male employers based all their particular judgements about career women on their assumptions about women in general. Even so, I was surprised, in looking for interviewees and setting up interviews, how many women there are now in positions of power and patronage in the business system. The top 200 British companies may have only twenty-nine female directors between them on their boards, but in 1980 there was only one – and there are now significant numbers of women ready and able to move into those top jobs.

The youngest woman I talked to was twenty-seven, the oldest fifty-nine. Some have university degrees; some left school without even an O level pass; some were brought up to expect only marriage and housework.

Most are working in London and the South-East, but I talked to successful businesswomen in the North-West, the North-East, and the West Midlands as well. Not one was born with the proverbial silver spoon. Only one had any specific intention when she left school of going into business; most had no clear idea of what they wanted to do or who they wanted to be. A few viewed the world of commercial work with horror, and pity for those who had to get to the office by nine every morning. The who, the what, the why, and the how of these women's careers and lives, that's what I wanted to learn. *Are* they different? I have changed their names to preserve their anonymity, because they were speaking very openly and personally, not as company representatives. In the process of answering my questions, they illuminate the much broader social and political context we all inhabit. But these are women who have made, and will continue to make, a difference to all our lives.

Is eternally springing hope making me overoptimistic about our future? I don't think so. As it is, though progress often seems slow, we have actually come a long way in a mere twenty years. As Treasury Minister Gillian Shephard says: 'Young women today are quite different from the way we were. They are wonderful, and we have made them. We don't need to be afraid of them. We should be proud of ourselves.'

And I believe that business, even in recession, is still the aspect of our culture most powerfully committed to expansion, to new ideas, to political initiatives, to contact with the outside world, in Europe, the USA and, increasingly, the developing Pacific Rim economies. The business culture is changing, and women are part of that change. And these are the women who are creating our future in their own image.

1

THE BUSINESS CULTURE:
OVER HIS DEAD BODY

THE point of listening is to learn. What I heard from the group of successful businesswomen who talked to me about themselves and their work has, I believe, some clear-cut messages to pass on about the shape of things to come for women as a whole. We are all well aware that we are living in a time of change in the relationship between the sexes, of redefinition of male and female roles.

Generation Gap

Even so, I found that one of the most startling things about my small sample of successful women is the evidence they provide of how much women's expectations have changed in a comparatively short time. There's just thirty years between the oldest and the youngest women I talked to. The older woman, you could say, was more ambitious, and certainly more pioneering. In forcing her way into a hierarchical corporate environment to get the basic knowledge and experience she needed to take a stab at a career in management, and, later, to start her own company, she had to ride roughshod over her upbringing to be wife and mother with perhaps a 'little job in her spare time', over the social expectations of other women, over male prejudice, and general bewilderment about just what kind of creature she was. The younger accepts as a *sine qua non* her choice of career, and her right to be wife and mother on her own terms.

Valerie, at thirty-eight a director of an executive recruitment company, has noticed the changes reflected in her clientele:

'Women now are a different breed from twenty years ago. For ten years at least, they've been getting used to expecting as of right a double life of career and family. University women now are much more confident, too. I think school and parental expectations have changed about what girls will want to do – i.e. have careers. My own parents were amazed when I wanted to go to university.'

There is a kind of emotional watershed between women above and below a line drawn at about the age of thirty-seven. Above the line, and the older woman's attitude to her career tends to involve an element of guilt – that she might not be what her husband or father would call a real woman, that she was selfish in doing something that gave her the fulfilment other women appear to find in motherhood. She still, to some extent, sees her own life and her success in terms of their effect on other people.

Young women have the confidence of their conviction that they can achieve what they want if they want to. Their independence is not compromised. They are not lazier than their older sisters, nor ungrateful for what has been achieved for them. But for the most part they have lost the self-doubt and ambivalence which come from older women's feelings that they are succeeding on – or in spite of – male sufferance.

This age line is very arbitrary. It is basically women's expectations about their role in life which have changed. According to Gillian Shephard, appointed Conservative Treasury Minister in her early forties, successful women, whatever their background, no longer see themselves as business hangers-on. She says this after a series of working breakfasts she held for businesswomen, mainly to find out how they were weathering recession:

'Young women are marvellous – a different species. They have no gender problems, and huge confidence. I think we have done this. The climate we have created has made them into the people they are. These are women who have no worries about putting a value on themselves.'

The Object of the Exercise

This leads to the second message which I heard coming over loud and clear from the successful women I talked to. It is a fundamental difference between older women and this new, different, species. Older women recognised that men and the male business culture were their opposition. Most support special treatment at work to promote women. This is not so for ambitious young women. They are not, on the whole, in favour of positive discrimination. They want to succeed on merit in open competition, and their aim is to achieve a genuinely gender-balanced business culture based on human ability and results. They have no doubts whatsoever that in such circumstances, they would more than hold their own. Positive discrimination, in their eyes, is a perpetuation of second-class status.

3

This is what they mean by 'the feminisation of the business culture'. That is not a proclamation of victory over a masculine-dominated system, and its replacement by practices based on cliché female virtues like submissiveness, obedience, and treating everyone at work like children and telling them to wrap up warm. Rather, it involves equal opportunity for everyone to explore their full potential at work. These women are not aiming to replace a male-dominated system with a female-dominated version. We're up against the lack of neutral language to encompass the evolutionary process here, because the challenge to the business culture is not simply a workplace process. It involves the way more women – and men – want to live outside work, too.

So another theme emerging from these women's lives is the way they are redefining womanhood. They are renegotiating the terms of their family relationships as well as the basis of work systems. We will see that for many successful women over about forty, having children was an either/or choice. Some of them were reluctant to give up the fulfilment they had achieved at work – or at least, were enjoying themselves enough not to have a sense of something missing. But many are married, or in longstanding relationships. Of these, most cut their teeth on a previous failed partnership. Their successful second tries were contracted in the context of two careers. The interests of the man's career do not outweigh those of the woman's. If it comes to a choice between them – say, over a job move – the compromise will be seen as a compromise, not as an automatic man's right to decide. Their changed business culture has altered their attitudes to relationships – they expect a partnership of equals. When there is a child – usually only one – parenthood involves both partners, first in the decision to have the baby, and then in bringing up the child.

A common quality among these women is their enthusiasm

for their working lives. In the 1960s and 1970s sense, they are liberated. Some women, who see the future they represent as daunting, might be chilled by the single-mindedness associated with their level of achievement. But when they define their ambition, they all say the same thing. They want elbow room to do their own thing. They want to make decisions which bring quantifiable results. They want to control their own and other people's lives – for the better. That's what they mean when they talk of changing the business culture.

The Politics of Women's Issues

You don't have to be a dyed-in-the-wool sceptic to doubt whether even a much larger group of women than my sample here have any hope whatsoever of bringing about such a vision. For a start, you say, men won't let them. For years now, we women have protested at the sexual discrimination we all experience. It is both explicit and implicit in our social system. We have discussed what we should do about it; what men should do; what the government should do – and complained when nothing anyone did brought about any fundamental change in the ingrained attitudes which protect the male-biased system. Neither logic nor legislation offered real solutions. Why should the chances of such change suddenly seem greater now?

One problem has been that genuine general agreement on an issue is not enough to bring about change. It does not matter how right the cause, nor how heinous the wrong. The issue has to be seen to be important. It must be something which wins or loses votes. Only then will it attract the power involved in bringing about change. Men on the whole, not surprisingly, have never seen equality of opportunity for women as important in this sense. But worse still women,

5

too, have suffered from a tendency not to see what they want as important in the general scale of things. Even Joanna Foster, chairman of the Equal Opportunities Commission, commenting on a 1991 report showing that senior and middle management in Britain are still dominated by men, acknowledged that the change in attitude necessary to bring about change 'is going to have to be brought about by men'.

Is there any sign that men – or, indeed, women – yet see women's progress as an 'important' issue? Well, a few male politicians promised that the nineties would be the Decade of Women. Government projections state that 85 per cent of new jobs during the decade will be taken by women, but recession has given the idea of such new jobs a hollow ring. After all, the Decade of Women implies something more than government promotional initiatives like Opportunity 2000, soothing words, or a few openings created in the service industries by fewer school leavers coming into the workforce – even if that drop is 30 per cent on the numbers in 1988. Judging by past performance, that will simply mean a continuation of the status quo – just more women still in low-paid, low-status jobs, earning 73 per cent of men's weekly wage.

Prospects of Change

Over the last twenty years, however, women's perception of themselves and each other has probably changed more than men's view of them. A study in 1977 by Walter Stephan and Dale Woolridge (*Sex Differences in Attributes for Task Performance*) suggests that more women than men saw women performing 'masculine' tasks as unconventional. Few women would feel that, let alone admit it, today. When you break the masculine mould in management systems, you release the female who looks after herself. She is the woman whom Dr

Christine Woesler de Panafieu, chief executive officer of the International Research Institute on Social Change (RISC), based in Paris, describes as the 'change-agent'. In this context, Dr de Panafieu calls British women 'the laggards of Europe'.

Her research throughout the European Community shows that British women are far less achievement-orientated than their European counterparts. The RISC Achievement Index 1989, where the European average is 100, shows that women in the UK score 79 compared with 106 in France, 93 in Germany, 103 in Italy, and 102 in Spain. Also, her findings show, both British society and British women lack the kind of new value system which would allow the jump into the post-materialistic society of Europe 1995. She says:

'The resistance [to change] of the British ideal of family life, together with the negative image of career women, is one important reason why women under forty-five are laggards compared with the general European trend. This situation, however, will not continue. Younger British women are quickly catching up with their European counterparts. They are very hedonistic and emotional, self-expressive and concerned with their own development; they are not very orientated to community or society, but they actively seek new ethical values. They are ready to take risks, cope with unforeseen situations, and very open-minded towards other European cultures, which is a new phenomenon for British citizens, who are mainly reluctant concerning European matters. But at the same time they share with other British women the tendency to leave social success and career-mindedness to men.

'Can one conclude that the young British women are a hope for the future? The answer is not easy to give because there exists an important population of young British

7

women living from day to day without any positive perspective.'

Change-Agents

Dr de Panafieu argues that to bring about change, there must be a critical mass of the kind of women who are catalysts for change. Half of European women, but only a third of British women, qualify as members of this change-agent group. Dr de Panafieu believes this is probably not enough for strong female modern perspectives when set against the two-thirds of British women who resist or reject change: 'For this situation to change will depend mainly on two circumstances: on the strength of the vital young British women to support ethical values and on a greater openness towards Europe which might broaden the horizon.'

On the face of it, the figures bear her out. A 1990 survey by the Hansard Society, *Women at the Top*, says that 81 per cent of British corporations have no women on their main holding boards, and under 25 per cent had more than one woman on any board. Women scarcely cause a numerical bump in the membership lists of the Institute of Directors, the British Institute of Management, or the Confederation of British Industry.

This seems to me of little significance in itself. I said earlier that it looks as if women who have succeeded in business are at last doing so on their own terms. They are no longer fighting men on men's terms. The CBI, the BIM, are part of that male system. Many successful women, running their own companies or at a senior level of management in corporations, will see such membership as irrelevant – just as regular attenders at the Institute of Directors would probably not race to join some of the many high-powered women's networks now up and running. It is surely encouraging that successful women remain aloof from these male preserves. It underlines the fact that although more women are working, and there are more (albeit not many) women in senior and influential jobs, the bastions of the *male* business system don't reflect them. Many ambitious women who set off along the corporate road find this culture uncongenial, and strike out on their own. National Westminster Bank, which has 30 per cent of the small-business banking market, took on 180,000 new business accounts in 1990. Sixty thousand of these were enterprises started by women. Businesswomen now represent a third of all business start-ups, compared with fewer than one in six ten years ago. The fact that they do not, apparently, see the CBI and its ilk as representative of business success strikes me as reason to hope that the culture itself is changing.

The Old Order Changeth . . .

According to the women on the spot, this change is a reality. Sally, now a main board director of the company which bought out her own business, says she started her management career in an old-style male-dominated hierarchy:

'The culture was becoming more feminised as more women rose to senior positions, but it was very slow. I set up my own business because I wanted to concentrate where I enjoyed work most, on the training side. I also wanted out of the politics, and the awful time-wasting that goes on in corporate hierarchies as people jockey for position. What I wanted to do in my own business was make sure people got the right end of the stick, and stop departments fighting each other instead of fighting the opposition – which is the kind of thing that goes on as part of the male system.'

Sheila, though she is a corporate finance director of a large manufacturing and retail company, moved from a senior position in another company because she found its 'masculine climate' counterproductive:

'I wanted to do my own show after seven years there – but for me that meant autonomy within a large company structure. I like to work in a situation where the buck stops somewhere, and the company I left was very matrix-orientated – run by committee. It was not a dynamic business because of the layers of decision-making which had to be gone through. My career path has always been on the principle of doing the best job I can and enjoying it, and having no more than a very general career plan, just to see where I could get. I feel comfortable with the more entrepreneurial businesses. It's a cultural thing. I don't like businesses with a strong hierarchical system.'

Why Is the Culture Changing?

Young and middle-aged women, who are proving their success in business management, now argue that the social and cultural changes which make the nineties the decade of women are already upon us. Sheila believes that society itself has become a catalyst for change:

'I wish I could say I thought women were changing the business culture. Unless there are some really radical changes in society (which may be forced by demographics) it's a slow haul. It's society, not women, who've got to change – people's rights, not women's. Attitudes are changing, but real change in society's pressure is about issues like having children and getting married if you didn't want to. I think that's changed. Then people who lived on their own

10

were queer, and now they're not. Society's acceptance of people who don't conform to the norm is a good sign, but it's society which must find a way to be flexible around people.'

The business culture reflects the changes in society, and changes in the business culture tend to lead to further changes in society. As to what has triggered this change – if it is not only the women themselves – Valerie, a main board director for a personnel recruitment chain, argues:

'The business culture is definitely changing, due to people's general awareness that they want more quality of working life rather than the women's effect. Employers in the last two years have been spending time looking at how they can make the organisation more amenable to women in management. That's partly because of demographics, but it's also because the culture where we all came in at 7.30 a.m. and went home very late at night wasn't working for anyone. People didn't stay. They came out and went independent or went to another organisation which didn't make such demands. There aren't enough women at senior positions yet to influence a change in the firm's culture.'

Then why are these changes taking place now? The kind of male business culture Valerie describes has operated for decades. Women, it seems, have not yet succeeded in colonising the male business bastions they have breached – there is unanimous agreement that there aren't yet enough women with the power to make that difference.

Not in the workplace, there aren't, but the quantum leap over the last twenty-five years or so in women's interpretation of womanhood has changed men. Ironically, it is some men who are apparently voluntarily abandoning the male-biased attitudes which have supported their workplace power base since the Industrial Revolution. Lorraine, thirty-five, a management consultant, says:

'If you look at guys running companies at the moment, most have had traditional male–female role differentiation. They're being made redundant. Their place is being taken by a new breed. Highly ambitious men in their thirties now don't experience that role difference. They marry girls they met at university, not their secretaries. They're dual-career couples. That's the time bomb. What will change these organisations is that men now have to negotiate with their wives on an equal basis about the way they live together. Men are not good at doing these things.'

Men In A State Of Flux

Indeed, many men are undergoing a metamorphosis whose significance they themselves are only just beginning to suspect. We are right to be suspicious of this. We are right to wonder what kind of trick this is. There is evidence, though, that men are changing their masculine tune, rather on the same principle as women in the 1950s bleached their hair because blondes had more fun. Men are realising that some women are beginning to have a better time than they do. Many women have reassessed their expectations in line with liberation. Suddenly, at least some women seem to be able to 'have it all'.

In contrast, the male ethos has remained rigid and constricting, as cumbersome as a hand-cranked lift in a skyscraper. Men are missing out.

On a personal level, some men are beginning to question the masculine blueprint they must follow in order to become men. This construct forced them early in their lives to suppress the potentially rewarding 'emotional' side of human nature. Masculinity is something they had to learn – and are now trying to 'unlearn' . . .

There are several reasons why this redefinition of masculinity should be happening now. On a business level, men are being forced to accept that the traditional male-devised and masculine-friendly hierarchical work system has been found wanting against international competition. The decline in traditional 'male' manufacturing industry based on physique is a contributory factor. Massive unemployment has forced men to question the role of work in perpetuating the clichés of masculine identity. Men without work become invisible, stripped of purpose and sense of self. This effect spills over into their family structures – particularly where their wives could find it comparatively easier than they do to get work in new service industries. Women's earnings became an essential part of the family budget, altering men's perception of themselves as sole breadwinner and head of the family.

Also, new technology has made the skills and experience of older men redundant in the face of a computer culture they feel is alien, and younger people in the workforce are now second-generation graduates of a comprehensive education system where the principle of sexual desegregation is a norm. And, of course, the women younger men meet and live with have independent expectations and demands which are not compatible with traditional male assumptions.

Nor is it coincidental that men, in significant numbers, are becoming aware of the inadequacies of masculinity. The American Robert Bly, in his 1991 US bestseller *Iron John: A Book About Men*, describes how the modern father in Western cultures is failing to provide his sons with a masculine blueprint. He cites increasing numbers of single-parent families and the corporate system which leaves a man little time outside work for his family as reasons for this lack of contact between 'absentee' fathers and sons. It is true, too, that the 'feminine' construct which the boy has to reject in order to become 'masculine' has changed enormously in the last three decades. Women as single parents, women as sole breadwinners, women working, highly educated and professionally qualified women, have all blurred the traditional distinctions between the two blueprints.

Thus society is suddenly faced with a perception of masculinity as distorted as its earlier concept of femininity. More men can now allow themselves to have emotions – some can even show them in public. Janet, head of her own market research company, which is now big enough to have a takeover bid administered by a top merchant bank, describes an incident she found heartening:

> 'I was at a meeting in the City this morning where a man of forty turned to his boss and said he would like time off to look after his kids built into the timetable of the project we were discussing. No one even blinked. He wouldn't even have said it two years ago. It would have cost him any chance of progress. It shows male values are changing . . .'

Male Corporate Bastions Crumbling

New men and househusbands, one-parent families, even mortgages depending on double incomes, are all part of a process of social change which involves a rethink of the whole concept of masculinity. So far, trial redefinitions of what male and masculine involves have tended to become social cul-de-sacs, but the redefinition process has started a questioning of the very 'male' hierarchical structures designed to protect the perception of masculinity (ruthless, competitive, authoritarian) on which the traditional corporate ladder rests. Peter, a personnel consultant and counsellor, says:

'Men are beginning to realise that their prizes are lethal. It's a process which goes back, for me, to *The Female Eunuch*. The simple message there was that femininity is a cultural contrivance – but it led me to think that so is masculinity. A boy has to learn to be masculine. Most of a child's sensitivities come from his primary parent, almost always his mother. But a boy knows quite early that in order to become a proper man, he must invent masculinity for himself. The first step is to break with your mother. All boys' culture is to do with putting down girls. Masculinity is based on asserting yourself against and above other people. I suppose I realised that male contempt for the feminine comes from a boy's need to reject his mother, but after reading Germaine Greer I understood that we men weren't stuck with the narrow, arid script of masculinity and femininity any more than women were.

'I've worked for and with men and women, and I can see that the dumb thing about men is that they're afraid of emotional content – sitting and listening – and unused to expressing emotional complexity. Remember that Joseph Heller quote: "Even as he soared like an eagle, he was falling to bits"? What's happening in our society now is that men are beginning to realise that their prizes are lethal.'

The Emerging Culture

The men who are falling to bits are finding masculinity sterile. It offers no shoots for new growth. On the contrary, womanhood, in a state of flux since the 1960s, offers an expanding and experimental avenue for new modes of living. Valerie, whose work in recruitment gives her ample opportunity to assess male motivations, is now convinced that the masculine business culture is doomed:

'Change has really come about because the demand for more quality of working life is coming from men who have got to senior positions in their forties and are realising there must be more to life than working their socks off, basically. They're coming to realise this quicker because new technology, etc., has catapulted them to power, while former senior management has been made redundant. These younger senior men want to know when they can see their kids, or their second family, because most of them are on second family by now. They got promoted to senior positions younger. Twenty years ago, they'd have got there in time to plan for retirement. Now they get a buzz from power for a couple of years, but they've still got the rest of their working lives to get through.'

Lisa, in her late twenties, a director of an advertising agency handling corporate clients from international banks to privatisation flotations, is working part-time until her eighteen-month-old daughter goes to school. She describes the effect of a recent change of male attitude at the top of the company:

'Company policy is based on the personalities at the top. Three years ago the two top men here were divorced and going through the bimbo stage. They took clients on horrible male nights out which excluded women because ordinary intelligent professional women and teenage dollies don't mix.

'Both of them have just got married to very nice women. It's had a very definite effect on the agency. It's a much more family atmosphere. The chief executive showed an interest when I took my baby to work one day because his wife is pregnant. That's why I've been able to do my job on a part-time basis – it's acceptable now, but if I'd got pregnant in his Jack the Lad phase, it would have been different. There are two other directors who are married and have affairs, and they're the ones who had a problem with my part-time. The business is their excuse and cover for their single lifestyle, and they don't want any overlap between family life and work. But suddenly they're out of tune with the company ethos, and because they're not comfortable, they're not particularly efficient.'

How Men React

Pragmatism, though, has always been a building block of the male persona. Men may have seen the writing on the wall for macho masculinity, but they need to see positive advantage to justify the radical change in adopting more humane principles.

They are finding that they do gain from the changes in management style women bring with them into the work-place. Nevertheless, women will need to see, before we can believe, any real shift in attitude which does not ultimately seek to exclude us. To make any fundamental change in social and cultural systems, the redefinition of masculinity must be a process of evolution, not a flash-in-the-pan conversion. Women's priorities must be built into the system – otherwise, how can we be sure that any changes in corporate policy associated with the female approach will be permanent and irreversible?

Ellen, training and personnel director of a national catering organisation, feels that men are confused about their role in current management theory:

'We have a lot of women operating as junior managers. They get stuck at a certain point in their careers – something to do with the shape of the organisation, which is a pyramid, and very steep at the top. As a main board director, I get asked to analyse why this happens, and defend the organisation's position both internally and externally on this issue. I refuse to do it. I say if they want that kind of analysis, I'm not the best person to do it. Actually, it's quite a difficult thing to say because I'm not being co-operative, I'm not supporting other women. But once you do it you become known as the resident expert on women, which has nothing to do with my actual job. That means that when they're not sure what the specific reaction to a woman's issue will be, they dump it on me and marginalise both the issue and me.

'It's depressing that the concept of "women's professions" does debase certain jobs. The evidence is overwhelming. Go into a building society and all the staff are women except the manager. And male nurses don't become matrons, they're nursing administrators – that's where I see little progress in women asserting themselves.'

But only five years ago, Ellen would not have been in a position to assert her right *not* to become the company's resident troubleshooter for women.

There are examples of cultural change in specific businesses which give cause for confidence. Take one British information technology group which for years has served as the epitome of classic male hierarchical management systems. Michael – formerly personnel director, now head of training – went through an epiphany when he worked on secondment to a charitable trust in the late 1980s. This converted him to the cause of equal opportunities, but he acknowledges that it is a change in the business culture as a whole which has allowed him to establish a genuine shift in the company ethos to embrace what he calls 'the feminine qualities of intuition, emotions, feelings, peacemaking'. He describes what has happened in his company:

'The culture has changed, predominantly in men's attitude. There aren't yet enough senior women to make changes – and often we've found that established senior women have a negative attitude to pushing for other women. They feel they got where they are without special help, so why shouldn't everyone else? But unofficially we do discriminate in favour of women. We will give a woman a place on a course in preference to a man – in our own interests. We've found it better to have women on a course rather than all-male. The women have a more open approach, and sort of give men permission to be open.

'There's a growing realisation now that women first-line managers (who have twelve specialists reporting to them) can be just as good in producing results, and yes, they may do it in different ways, and not adapt the traditional management role. That traditional role is all bound up with the systems in the company which are reward-based – assessments and salary depend on rating. The managers within the system don't get involved with work on feelings levels or spend more time than they have to on relationships with people. The attitude is "don't give me trouble and you'll do OK". It may be women don't like those systems, but things in society as a whole are changing, and with a number of young people in the company the system is starting to break down – or rather, it's being pushed aside as irrelevant. So I think the idea of hope and reward is no longer as significant as interest in challenge and the interest of the job and the quality of the job; being open and direct rather than competing. This is the case with people in general in the company, but I must say it marries up more closely with the outlook of a woman than a man. I do think, though, that it's society as a whole which is changing the corporate culture, but the changes do play more to the strengths of women, and will give them a better chance.'

This demonstrates a very fundamental attitude change in that particular company, but one swallow doesn't make a summer. Of course there are still a number of major corporate employers who would find it difficult to be adaptable even if Boadicea staged a comeback. Michael's company is international, based in the South-East. But even in the most intransigent male-chauvinist hierarchies – particularly in the provinces, which tend to be out of touch with international trends – the need to keep in touch with the competition is leading to pressure from within for changes in management policy. Julie is a main board director of a subsidiary company within a privatised industrial monopoly. Before coming to work at the London headquarters, she worked for the same employer in the Midlands and the North:

'I came in as a graduate management trainee. I couldn't believe the attitudes of the men who were managers in the provinces. It was not just that they did everything they could to limit my operations to making tea or answering enquiries. There was no way men like that were ever going to see the need for change.'

But Julie believes that even in her company's provincial offices, that kind of man is now obsolete. He was not condemned only for his chauvinism, but also because he was inefficient. Julie's experience suggests that even the most recalcitrant masculine-dominated structure *is* being forced to adjust in order to survive:

'When I came in, thirteen years ago, the business was very civil-service based, very rank-conscious, very hierarchical, very bureaucratic, with endless rulebooks. People making a decision would look up the rulebook rather than applying their own common sense within general guidelines. We're partly through the latest reorganisation now, which is very much the result of changing attitudes.

'But though we have many more women, and the men are getting more used to it, women haven't reached the critical-mass point. We have between 170,000 and 180,000 employees, and 14 per cent overall are women. Most promotion is from within, so the proportion of women gets lower the higher you get. There are two crucial points of movement – from being a non-manager to being a manager, and from mid to senior management. About two years ago we had a total-equality initiative, and a lot of senior management posts were put in with an extended selection procedure. Extended selection means you kill the subjective bias of the anti-women, even if their prejudice is subconscious, and a large number of women were successful.

'Our chairman and the personnel director are very pro equal opportunity. The managing director's not sure. But there are high-level people throughout the operation who don't understand it, and we have to try to change their entrenched attitudes. We've changed the promotion structure, where formerly you could be promoted to certain jobs only if you were already in certain grades or hierarchies. Secretaries weren't eligible for promotion, for example. One of the things I did was sweep all that away.

'The most difficult thing to crack is changing male attitudes and getting across that regardless of their personal opinions, it's (a) business policy and (b) the law that we don't discriminate against women. But reasons can be found, even if it is against the law.'

Can Change Stick?

Moves like this in such a traditional company help to build confidence that real cultural change is under way in the corporate structure. Whether these changes are down to corporate self-interest or enlightenment imposed from outside – by social or political imperatives, for instance – both these examples suggest that aspiring women managers have an unprecedented opportunity of benefiting from what is happening. Any woman over thirty-five and worth her feminist salt will blow a raspberry at that, of course – *plus ça change*, and all that – except that the difference this time is that male self-interest is also behind change. There is no question that any business policy shift in favour of women is an altruistic act on the part of men. Men are not being kind. They are fighting for survival. Given the capitalist framework, their motives are encouragingly selfish. Because this is so, we can be more inclined to give them credence. Nor need we fear that such changes are a flash in the pan. The social factors which are changing men's concepts of their own masculinity are now irreversible. They have gone too far to change now. There is no prospect of resuscitating manufacturing industries in their old forms, with their reliance on physical strength. New industries – computer technologies, communications, financial services – have little inbuilt gender bias.

The Part Women Play

This is where women are becoming catalysts. Women themselves are not looking for an exclusively female business environment. As I said earlier, in the context of positive discrimination, most want to aspire to standards which incorporate the best of both worlds. They want a business culture which recognises that they are evolving a new and much broader definition of womanhood. Where men are finding themselves limited by the traditional concept of masculinity, women are finding that the process of breaking away from the restrictions of traditional ideas of womanhood still has a long way to go before gender becomes incidental. While men have been preserving and conserving, women have been developing and evolving alternative management styles to which men are now looking for management solutions. As I've said, women are different now. There is no chance at all of packing career women *en masse* back to the kitchen sink. We like working outside the home. Women are proving themselves very good at what they do. Change-agent women, if they have children, are in more control of motherhood and career. It is now such women who have genuine choice. It took some winning, and they are not going to allow anyone else to make that choice for them.

At the same time, the economic and industrial state of the nation has demonstrated that male-dominated management style is inadequate. Michael, the training director of the computer combine, like many of his opposite numbers in large new-technology companies, has a mandate from his chief executive to seek solutions to the discredited and inadequate male-dominated management systems. They agree that these solutions play to the strengths of women:

'We're an American company, and we first made an effort to do something about increasing the numbers of women when there was corporate pressure from the US. There was no pressure from within the company, but in any case it just didn't make sense to have as few women as we did. First we made an effort in terms of selection, putting more emphasis on objectivity and individual ability, but saying we should hire more women. We never set quotas, as in the US, but over the process of a few years our graduate intake is now 30 to 35 per cent women. It hasn't made that much effect on manager numbers yet; we still have only 5 per cent women. But it has had an effect on sales, which is the key area. I remember a branch manager saying he'd like more women, but the customers wouldn't wear it. That's proved nonsense, and now 25 per cent of our salesmen are women. I mean salesmen, too – we started out calling everyone sales representatives as we got more women, but now we've all gone back to salesmen. We've also got more women on the engineering side for the first time as the job changed from wires and rivets towards software.

'In terms of managers, at first there was a lot of reluctance from the company. But now, in recruiting graduates, we look for a broad spectrum of qualities like ability to relate to people, communicate well, openness, flexibility in outlook, rather than specific science qualifications, and these are all qualities associated with women.

'Now I've seen the ambition and corporate drive in young women. They are interested in the corporate structure as it is now. The change has been quite sudden, and I put it down to our perception of women. We've always had a high degree of commitment and job satisfaction in the company, but we didn't associate it with women. Now we can see they do have corporate drive and are committed. Now we have senior women managers in personnel, marketing, finance, and one in customer engineering. I wouldn't rule out a woman chairman – probably from marketing.

'I was talking to a group recently about management styles, and said women were successful in employing different styles. And this older manager said: "Oh, they're showing their tits, are they? Ha ha!" I don't think a young man would actually say this, and I still find it incredible. It stems from male insecurity and desire to keep management closed as a cosy group.'

The Survival Imperative

British business has not accepted even this degree of female influence without a struggle. Men in general are no more willing to relinquish their built-in dominance in the workplace than many women were to abandon the refuge of female dependence. It's true that after the bloodletting in manufacturing industry in the early 1980s, when well over a million workers in nationalised industries lost their jobs in rationalisation progammes, British management in turn suffered some kind of *crise*. Innovative managers tried to leaven the lump by forcing a flow of information moving upwards and downwards to get some sign of life from business structures frozen in masculine hierarchical modes; hence management experiments aimed at increasing co-operation between boss and worker – quality circles, team briefings, and the rest. But such initiatives tended to concentrate on applying a cosmetic improvement to the old – implicitly masculine – system built on self-interested individuals competing with each other; on aggression, confrontation and autocracy. In short, male interpretations of women's approach to getting their own way were slapped on a business structure which was based on rejection of women. The result was as unconvincing as men in drag. There was certainly little benefit to women intended in any of these attempts to salvage male pride. Anyway, such changes came too little and too late to save the traditional systems. Effectively, by the end of the 1980s, they had broken down. Now, according to Sally:

'A lot of management training and theory now are in fact the feminine way of doing things. Traditional practice was strong, authoritative, combative, and now what a lot of training does is advocate communication and leading by example. We're training for existing male hierarchies, but the way training operates is to look at what successful managers do. Distil that, and we can say that's the magic. And successful managers tend to do it the feminine way, if you like. We can all be dominant and gentle, though in many people that's out of balance. In most successful people they are both there in equal measure. Men who allow their feminine side to surface are the better managers for it.'

In academia, too, current management thinking is moving away from the idea of groups of insulated individuals and towards management 'types' as team players. Dr Meredith Belbin, of the Industrial Training Research Unit at Cambridge, identifies individual roles as they are crucial to a successful team. Managers have their formal job titles, but they also perform a variety of 'personality team roles' – the ideas person, the stickler for detail, the diplomat, the gaudy fixer, the bully galvaniser. Dr Belbin has worked out psychometric tests – literally measurements of the psyche, or a kind of executive Richter scale to identify personality traits – and on the basis of these findings it is possible to predict accurately the relative performance of differently composed teams.

Here we have a management dénouement close to the gender balance the ambitious younger women in my sample say they want to achieve – equal, but different.

The potential is there. Psychometric tests applied to a group of male and female high-fliers for the now defunct *Business* magazine by the Vocational Guidance Association in July 1991 were carefully designed not to show that men and women were 'better' than each other, but to 'trace and display managerial traits and aptitudes'. When the guinea pigs' answers to nearly 20,000 questions had been put through the VCA computer, it was found that 'men and women executives have more talents in common than most people imagine – and some considerable managerial differences, too.'

Some of the findings were surprising. Women, for instance, pay more attention to detail, but are less democratic. They also emerged as prepared to make decisions of their own, and this ability to act without feeling a need to consult others 'is in marked contrast to men, who feel obliged to favour the group decision'. Two basic reasons emerged why women do not make it to the top: they do not know how exceptional they are; and they lack confidence.

Psychometrically, though, it is people who are different, not the sexes. Lisa, for example, agrees with the result of psychometric testing: that her *raison d'être* is 99 per cent the pursuit of power, even though this strikes even her as not typically female: 'It's true. I hope I wouldn't stamp on anyone to get it, but I couldn't be sure I wouldn't.' Michael, on the other hand, is an ace communicator, with little 'typically masculine' personal drive. 'I don't think there's much difference between men and women,' Lisa says. 'It's people who are very different.'

What Price Gender Balance Now?

The evolution of the concept of a gender-balanced human business culture is a powerful theme for the younger women I talked to. Older women are more sceptical. 'Sexuality was part of the business process when I started,' says Janet. She adds:

> 'I have just been in the United States, taking part in various high-level business meetings about an international project my firm is working on. The young women there were an eye-opener. There was absolutely no flirting at all.
>
> 'When I was first in management, there was always an element of flirtatiousness between the few women and our men colleagues. It didn't mean anything – it was how we communicated. But younger women don't do it. My daughter, for instance, is a junior hospital doctor. A consultant told her he liked something she was wearing. She said: "Yes, I like your suit, too. Now can we get back to the job in hand." Wow! We wouldn't have dared take such a risk, for one thing.'

Ethnic Minority Changes

Many women – older successful women, for example – feel that they need an element of sexuality in their business style actually to give them the confidence of familiar ground. There is also the point – if we agree that many women *are* different from the way they were twenty years ago – that the vast majority of women have adjusted their expectations about what being female makes possible. This may be something high-flying and successful women take for granted, but many more may still need a kind of permission from peer-group women before they step away from the security of traditional role definition.

Take women from ethnic minorities, for instance, who have found the odds stacked against an equal opportunity of climbing the corporate hierarchical ladder in a strongly male system. They also are responding to the new entrepreneurial business climate as it begins to embrace new priorities. In the multicultural society Britain pretends to be, women from ethnic minorities are participating in changing their traditional constructs of womanhood through workplace success. Julie, whose company employs thousands of female workers, has found that women from ethnic minorities, particularly Asian women, see their own ambition as unwomanly:

'They think it's unfeminine to push themselves forward because in their culture women are subservient. In some of our offices Asian women did not want to be promoted to positions where they would be supervising men. The Asian men didn't want it either.'

But according to Claire Hynes of the Black British magazine *The Voice*, more black women than ever before are joining the enterprise culture:

'Around 40 per cent of black businesses are now being set up by African-Caribbean women, which is slightly higher than the figure for white women's input in white businesses.

'Black women are moving into interesting new areas of business – to a greater extent than their male counterparts. They are moving away from traditional areas of business and setting up in areas like food processing, book publishing, fashion designing and the music industry.

'Five years ago, black women made up fewer than one in four black businesspeople, and the vast majority were involved in trades like hairdressing, catering and dressmaking. There is also anecdotal evidence that the failure rate of businesses run by these women is much lower than the rate for black men.'

The Thin End of the Wedge

Misplaced optimism can prove painful, and women are well aware of that. Change-agent women in business are the thin end of a wedge, and how far they succeed in cracking open the male structure and getting in through the gaps will probably depend on the pressure from the women behind them. Lynda Gratton, Assistant Professor at the London Business School, sounds a cautious note:

'We are in the top ten UK business schools. It's our job to train managers. We do this in two ways – as MBA [Master of Business Administration] students, and people in organisations who come for executive development courses.

'Thirty per cent of our MBA students are women. We receive significantly fewer female applicants, and though we don't positively discriminate, we are more likely to bring in women because those who do apply have stronger CVs. The area we're worried about is executive development. On those courses we have 10 per cent women, and lower on some.

'The problem is that to get to the top of an organisation you have to have gone through some sort of management education process, and women are not being nominated for that. In 1989 we set up a working party to look at women in management education. One issue we looked at was how to ensure, if we did increase numbers, that women's experience was more positive than it is at the moment, and help women work together with men. Women will say it's actually bloody awful being the only woman in a group of twenty men – an experience I have continually – and it wears you down. They go to the pub and drink lots of beer (especially the British managers; the Europeans are a bit more sophisticated). When I started teaching here, I taught a course for a large British multinational. On the first day I walked in and they said, "Hallo, darling, you teaching us today? What's a girl like you doing as a professor?" '

The difference in the last few years – very few: two or three – is that Lynda is now the one with the power over those men. Her judgements could affect their promotion prospects with their firm, so she could make any residual male chauvinism tell against them in their careers.

2

WHY THEY ARE
THE WAY THEY ARE

UNTIL recently, women's experience of management success has played little or no part in representations of how business works. The male culture was the norm because it was the only one available for study. To find out how women may change the business culture, we need to know more about what makes businesswomen tick.

The Genetic Difference

The way people talk about masculine and feminine management style in the corporate structure often assumes that the difference is genetic. Michael, who lectures on management students as part of his job, believes there is some truth in this. Certainly at birth there is a difference:

'Boys are born with bigger right sides to their brains. That's the side which controls spatial ability. The right side of the brain is the mathematical, rational side. Girls have bigger left hemispheres, controlling language. That's the artistic, emotional, integrated side.

'Research into the way children play shows that boys play competitive games. Girls don't play the kinds of games which have winners and losers. Boys exclude newcomers, but will include one if he can show he is useful. Girls are curious about newcomers, but will exclude them if subsequently they don't fit in.'

In her book *You Just Don't Understand: Women and Men in Conversation*, Deborah Tannen, Professor of Linguistics at Georgetown University in Washington DC, quotes instances of early differences between the sexes. She says that boys tend to play outside in large groups that are hierarchically structured: they have a leader who tells others what to do and how to do it. Boys play games with winners and losers and elaborate systems of rules, and they boast about their skills and argue about who is best at what.

Girls, on the other hand, play in small groups or pairs. Professor Tannen writes:

The centre of a girl's social life is a best friend. Within the group, intimacy is key: Differentiation is measured by relative closeness. In their most frequent games, such as jump rope and hopscotch, everyone gets a turn. Many of their activities (such as playing house) do not have winners or losers. Though some girls are certainly more skilled than others, girls are expected not to boast about it, or show that they think they are better than the others. Girls don't give orders. They express their preferences as suggestions, and suggestions are likely to be accepted ... girls are not accustomed to jockeying for status in an obvious way; they are more concerned that they be liked.

Women's Style

Treasury Minister Gillian Shephard argues that whether or not the difference is significant or measurable, women perceive themselves as different from men in management style and intention:

'Initially I had a few misgivings about looking particularly at women in business, but I feel we've gone past the "you must not single out women" mode, and that was borne out by what I learned. There is a woman's style of management – and incidentally, in some instances it has helped the business survive in the current climate.

'Asked if they felt there was anything in the way they ran the business which differentiated them from men's style, some said they came out of corporations because they felt they were very clubby – fairly exclusive – and it was more difficult for them to get there and make money because they had to work through the clubs and layers. Once they were liberated from that, they were very successful.

'Those who felt they worked in a definite woman's style said they ran their companies in a democratic way. It came naturally to them, even without personnel officers telling them it was the right thing to do. They were interested in the individuals, in the circumstances of the people who worked for them. And they also felt compelled to ask employees their opinion of change without it being laid down in the manual.

'I think they were very careful about research for future prospects. This did not necessarily differentiate them from men, but some did say they had taken particular trouble to see the way trends were moving, and hadn't felt that this was so when they worked in larger, more male-dominated organisations, where the market is seen as a juggernaut which just steams on. These women actually struck me as more forward-looking and possibly more cautious than most men – maybe they were less likely to take risks, and planned more. One, who had weathered several recessions over the years, said, "There's a lot of money to be made in a recession. I usually pick up derelict land myself." A headhunter said she had survived because it was obvious something was going to go wrong and so she didn't go into the bubble industries, just stuck to established industrial business.'

Extraordinary Women

In general, successful women feel that there is very little difference in performance between men and women. Back in 1970, an article in the *Journal of Counselling Psychology* by the psychologist Harmon found that the identity of female managers (as opposed to women who were not managers) was related to self-status, rather than to the achievements of father, husband or brother. This is significant only in that it shows – at a time when the older women I talked to were already well launched on running their own businesses – how unquestionably the female norm was defined by the status of the men associated with her. So can we assume that women who are managers have characteristics which differ from those of other women?

I don't think that the drive for self-status provides sufficient definition – surely it was not exclusive to women in business even then. In 1848, the pioneering American feminist Eliza-beth Cady Stanton said: 'Put down in capital letters: Self-development is a higher duty than self-sacrifice.' In the context of a concept of womanhood which defined business success as unfeminine, both these female imperatives may have been irreconcilable. The drive to self-development pushes an ambitious woman on, even though she has sufficient income and the satisfaction of doing a job she enjoys, towards a position of power and responsibility where, among other things, she finds that her decisions can make or break other people's lives. In this she would appear, in Deborah Tannen's terms, to be acting against the 'feminine' nature findings of the psychometric tests carried out for *Business* magazine – 'some of the best women managers do not achieve their full potential in business because they do not know how exceptional they are'. And Harmon's research concluded that 'the overwhelming majority of women managers saw themselves as the same as other people, though actually they are one among few'. I think it is important, in trying to understand what makes senior women managers tick, to realise that they do not see themselves as out of the ordinary. Very senior and successful women are dominated by the feeling that they share interests with other people. Unlike men, they seem not to be driven to prove their distinction.

Here again, there is a problem about the use of words. 'Ordinary' is synonymous with 'normal': with hanging in, not out. This concept is fundamental to understanding what women want to achieve when they take charge.

Dounne set up and runs her own factory, making her 'Gramma's Pepper Sauces', based on her West Indian grandmother's herbal recipes. She supplies a market ranging from Harrods and Fortnum and Mason to selected Tesco and Safeway supermarkets. She believes that her 'ordinariness' is the basis of her success:

'All women, black and white, undervalue themselves because tradition has categorised them as second-class people. I recognised that because I was what most women are, a good mother and wife, I could be a good manager. I do not have to learn how to take responsibility, how to pay attention, always be in demand. An ordinary mother always wants her kids' lives to be better than hers, so being with our children, we are in step with time more than men are.'

It's easy enough, too, to identify the 'ordinary' in, say, Andrea, also a divorced housewife and mother, who started her own now successful import/export business. She was brought up deliberately not to work. She was moulded to a female norm: her future lay in the support of a decent bread-winner and the raising of children. She was not even expected to marry for love; she should marry a man who would give the children the best possible start in life. It was only after her divorce, and when she had given up any realistic hope of getting married again, that she decided she must find some-thing useful to do for the rest of her life. She set up in business because she couldn't think of anything else she could do:

'I did it because of a relationship I couldn't break or do anything with. I'd been brought up to get married and have children. The decision to start a business was almost a dare. I told the man of my plan, thinking he'd say don't do that, marry me. He didn't. He said he thought it sounded interesting. So I grumbled and he said get on with it. It was sink or swim. The pretence was financial independence, which would enable me to make decisions which had nothing to do with my anxieties about how we'd live. I never thought I'd go on with it. But it was like eating a box of chocolates – you just go on one step at a time.'

You can recognise this 'ordinariness' in Sarah, who started out on the process of becoming chief executive of a retailing group because she broke her engagement and needed to move away from her home because she kept bumping into her jilted fiancé.

And even the women who were always extraordinary never saw themselves as anything outside the norm. Take Sheila, daughter of a miner's widow in a close-knit, poor, rural community, but at an early age destined for academic distinction as an astrophysicist. It was too rarefied for her. In her third year at Oxford, she decided that what she really wanted was a more ordinary career. She wanted to use her numeracy. She went into business. She is now finance director of a company with an annual turnover of £150 million.

Even so, she sees herself as perfectly ordinary. Astrophysics is a qualification, not a characteristic. She is still the swot from a close-knit mining village, where her friends still are.

This perception of themselves may, of course, be part of these women's management style. They want to make ordinariness the norm as part of a general ethos they are working to achieve. If I labour this point, it's because I think it's important for all women to see their close connection with these high-flying change-agents if we are all to benefit from their achievements. These women are not aliens.

Lorraine, who commands £1,500 a day as a consultant, watches her extraordinary self with amazement from the point of view of the ordinary person she says she is:

'If I look at the people who were at school with me, I wasn't particularly talented. I do think that being a working woman has a major impact on your confidence and how you present yourself. But other women as talented as I am do all sorts of jobs, and don't have what's called success. If I'm at a mums' party, we all seem to be the same, and I know that in ten minutes' time I'm going to be getting into

a taxi and minutes later I'll be standing in front of the board
of a multinational and giving them advice. And I don't
know why I'm doing that and not them.'

Feeling that she was losing touch with 'ordinary' issues, Anne
has given up her senior management job to have a baby, with
the deliberate intention of reviving bonds with the community
at large:

'I was finding that because of the concentration at work
and the office, I had lost touch with important aspects of
society. These are aspects of community life a child gives
you access to – education and welfare, things like that. I
felt work wasn't giving me access to the real world, and I
wanted to get back into the construction of society.'

All these extraordinary women also live full domestic lives
as well as the added dimension of business success – and 'live'
means hands-on involvement, not lip service. Traditionally,
this is a fundamental difference between men and women –
though, as we saw in Chapter 1, men are increasingly seeking
access to the emotional and community life ordinary women
take for granted. Even Sheila, astrophysicist turned finance
director, who admits that at present her work fills her life
after her marriage and other relationships failed, sees herself
as a person primarily as a participant in a home-based
community outside the office. She knows the local shop-
keepers. She takes part in local activities. She and her neigh-
bours are familiar with each other's kitchens. She regularly
goes to her old school reunions in the insular mining community where she grew up. She picks up with her childhood
friends where she left off to go to Oxford and a life quite
outside their experience. Some of them have never left rural
Derbyshire; she has just returned from her umpteenth trip to

Japan. 'There's no problem that they think I'm different. It's as though I'd never left. What I do at work doesn't mean anything to them. We just pick up and remember all the laughs we used to have,' she says.

Guilt and Isolation

Particularly among older women, there's often a niggling guilt involved in the gap they perceive in their own lives between the real ordinary them – the domestic wife and mother – and their extraordinary function outside the home as successful businesswomen. The two selves are at odds, and the guilt arises because the one they give priority is not necessarily the one those around her prefer. The old female construct of the selfless carer is at odds with her phoenix independent female identity. So Janet, head of a market research company, still feels guilty:

'I blame myself for the break-up of my first marriage. I expected to be able to be what he wanted – a wife and mother with a job as a hobby on the side. But I couldn't do it. I think I was not a good mother because the job had to come first so we could survive. And now I'm very much aware that my present husband is getting on and I should spend more time with him. Because of a business crisis, I had to tell him three days before we went on holiday that I couldn't go. I said I'd catch up, but I knew I wouldn't. And the business takes up so many evenings . . .'

Sarah feels that she is in danger of losing what she has in common with other people as success isolates her from them:

'I'm lonely. Married colleagues socialise with each other, but I don't get invited. Even before I was their boss, I was friendly with the guys, but didn't get invited as a peer. A difficult thing is that for a single person a lot of social life is through work. The higher you get, you have to drop people because you can't go to Edith's home to have coffee because Edna worries why you're not going to her house. It's not who you go with, it's who you don't that's the problem.

'I find it quite difficult to flirt now because it's such a way of life being me the businesswoman. I actually find it difficult to be flirty outside work. I definitely need a drink first. I'm so used to not using my femininity at work as the boss.'

Outsiders

By pursuing their unusual ambitions, these women risk becoming outsiders. According to psychological studies in the United States, women fear achievement as bringing isolation, being forced to stand apart. Many women may work in a public arena, and success may involve recognition from other people, but to get to the top a woman has to push herself forward, to stand out.

Another study, by psychologist Douglas LaBier, in his book *Modern Madness: The Emotional Fallout of Success*, examined mental and emotional health in the traditional male-biased corporate workplace. LaBier found that highly successful women were more emotionally disturbed than comparable men. The men became 'authoritarian and sadistic', but 'remained essentially true to their masculine identity'. But women, he claimed, affirmed nothing but a perverted sense of values, denying their femininity and becoming more and more empty inside.

This struck a chord with some of the successful older

women in my group. In the early stages of their careers, in very male-dominated corporate systems, they had surprised and worried themselves by the possibly inordinate ruthlessness they displayed when they felt under threat:

'At the time I was managing director of a subsidiary to the main company. When I was pregnant, I said I wanted to return in three months to the same job. This was 1960, and I was earning £3,300, which was good money then. They said I'd have to take a 10 per cent salary cut and be demoted to just a director.

'When I came back at the lower level, the way to conquer the new managing director was to have an affair with him, which I did. Then I got forty of our staff to resign and set up in competition.'

The younger women did not share this perception of the workplace as threatening. They do not see themselves as capable of overt ruthlessness. Lisa, director of an advertising agency, says: 'I am very ambitious. I want power to control my own life and other people's. But I hope not at any cost . . .' Younger women's lack of a sense of being threatened by the business culture – an aspect of confidence, perhaps? – even applies to their reaction to failure. Joan, who runs her own property management business, admits she cannot understand the attitude of young colleagues:

'They have this clinical way of dealing with everything. It's as though they feel they aren't personally implicated in what happens. I know this really young woman whose business failed. She was very upset, but quite differently from the way I was when I nearly went under. She didn't take any responsibility. She sacked all her staff, but what had happened had happened. She didn't accept any blame.

She just picked herself up and started again. She didn't seem to have lost any confidence in *herself*. She'd worked hard and she'd been successful for a bit, so she couldn't be to blame.'

Motivation

This is an aspect of the way women perceive their role as managers. To the majority of corporate men, motivation is a discrete quality. It describes the personal drive to move upwards and onwards, away from other men. Senior women, on the other hand, mean something else by it. In trying to show what they do mean, it may help to understand something about what originally drives them into risking isolation by putting themselves through a constant career prospect of trial and tribulation.

Is it a factor of education? There appears to be no common educational bond between these successful women. Sheila and Sally, the managing director of a training company, both think that going to a single-sex school was an advantage. 'I know a number of girls who get very distracted in mixed schools,' Sally says. Others left school without O and A levels. Of them all, only Valerie had decided by the time she left school that she wanted to go into business, and exactly what she wanted to achieve: 'I intended to be a main board director by the time I was thirty-five.' The others unanimously agree that they expected to work outside the home as well as to marry and have children. But they were not specific about what work they would like to do; nor did they expect to be any different from their contemporaries at school.

It is only fair to mention, though, before accepting these women's recollection of themselves as average and not particularly motivated, that they see today's students as comparatively less idealistic. For instance, Ellen, who lectures management students:

> 'A lot of women students now are very naive. I think non-British girls are more radical, but they all talk in terms of privileges and facilities rather than what they can contribute.'

Valerie, too:

> 'I think probably European students are less reactionary than some. They are not particularly strong in their views about anything. They're not looking to change the world. They want a good standard of living and to enjoy themselves. They may be green, but there aren't so many protest movements now. I don't think they jump on soap boxes so much as we did.'

This may possibly suggest that today's high-achieving women were not quite as nondescript and unfocused as they think they were. Or it could indicate that educational background and academic training are not powerful catalysts in subsequent career success.

Mothers

What really do seem to count, though, are mothers. Every successful woman I talked to finally ascribed her drive to succeed to her mother. Sheila is unequivocal:

> 'My father died when I was ten. My mother had to bring up me and my brother. She'd started work when she was fourteen, stopped when she married my father, and had to go back. He was a miner. I went to a girls' grammar school, where there was no peer pressure from boys. I've known

people who get intimidated by that. I went back to a reunion, and not one was in anything like my job. Most had given up work for children, or worked part-time.

'It was my mother made the difference. She didn't drive me, but she gave me support for what potential I had. A mining community in the North was very chauvinistic, very working-class, with strong pressure to stay with your roots. She always told me she knew I'd move on – I knew that through her from the age of about six. But she never gave me any feeling that I had to prove myself. She's proud of me, but I am of her. I've always wanted to be the person she wanted to be – honourable, honest, caring.'

Karen – who, as the head of a mixed school in the West Midlands, is one of the new breed of teachers-turned-education-managers – also feels that her success is the result of the role model her mother provided:

'I grew up in a totally female world, with no male role models at all. What that gave me was a great sense of the worth of women. It's silly little things, like being taught to wire up a plug in secondary school, and my mother had taught me that years before. She brought the coal in, did the gardening, supported me. It meant I've never had an image that there were things men did and things women did.'

Andrea, child of Jewish immigrants, was brought up to get married, but what she sees as her mother's legacy was a drive to provide her with a better life than her own. For Lisa, the happiness her mother got out of going to work came as a revelation:

'My father didn't want my mother to work, and she had no job until I was fifteen. Then she took a part-time job. I found her completely different after she went out to work. It gave her great confidence to be earning money for herself. She really enjoyed spending that money, more than anything she ever got from buying things with my father's money.'

The Wisdom of Mothers

All the successful businesswomen talked about their mothers with admiration as well as love. Only two mentioned their fathers as having any particular influence on their career path – except, perhaps, by their absence. Notwithstanding shifts in society – access to education, and the Women's Movement – what is interesting is that most of these mothers had in common men who had not fulfilled the traditional obligations which society places on husbands and fathers. Perhaps they had died, perhaps they ran off, or were simply not particularly successful men. But what all these successful daughters have in common is that they learned from their mothers – sometimes by example, sometimes by a process of osmosis, sometimes by repeated warnings – that they must stand on their own feet. They should not rely on a man as financial support, nor as a source of identity. They must take on the responsibility to control the environment in which they wanted to live. The alternative was to accept the imperfect muddle men had created for their mothers.

This involves proving – as in *im*proving – yourself. This may come out in the assumption many women make that they must be better than a man to succeed. It amounts to a duty, almost a compulsion, not to be dependent. These women did not want their mothers' lives. Their mothers – at the least unfulfilled, sometimes bitter – did not want their daughters to repeat an unsatisfying pattern: they cut the umbilical cord of traditional feminine convention to let their daughters go free. Sophie, a senior administrator for a trade union, suggests that not only have individual mothers inspired and projected their own successful daughters, but as role models they are responsible for opening the cage for an entire generation:

> 'What's happening is a younger generation of educated women with expectations of a career, and very conscious of the politics of that career. Equal Pay and other Acts are a fact of life to them. Then a lot of women in the 1960s went to redbricks, which opened up university to all classes. So you have mothers who actually worked themselves, were probably undervalued at work and resentful because of it. These young women are looking at their mothers' resentment and they're determined it won't happen to them. Having children was a thing you didn't do then if you wanted a career. Children were resented as enemies of promise. The mothers of these young women today are martyrs.'

Anger

Women, though, have to be careful of anger. Fear of men's anger against them is innate, because of physical disadvantages which mean they will always come off worst. Many ambitious women have absorbed anger from frustrated mothers. Many successful young businesswomen today knew instinctively of their mothers' resentment. These mothers were perhaps the first generation to lose faith in the masculine mystique and, furthermore, to have intimations that women could have done a better job. As educated and intelligent women, they made greater demands on men's emotional support, sensitivity and maturity – and found them gravely wanting. Often they saw their daughters as a source of hope for the future, whereas sons partook of the general male failure. Sheila's relationship with her mother illustrates the support mothers can give their daughters' ambitions:

'I was very lucky to have her as a mother. It wasn't in the least a competitive relationship between us – more us against the world. I was never driven, but supported to reach my potential. She always told me to plot my own way through life, to be independent and always make my own decisions.'

Lesley runs an independent TV production company. Her mother tried to steer her daughter away from the consequences of sex:

'She told me not to have children unless I really, really wanted to. When I said to her that then I'd miss out on the kind of wonderful relationship I have with her, she said, "How many mothers and daughters do you know who have a relationship like ours? Don't do it."'

Lesley's mother saw inept control of her sexuality – by marrying and having the child – as the reason for her own failure to compete successfully in the workplace. This is not unique. I remember a college friend of mine telling me how she would never marry or have a longstanding relationship with a man because of something her mother had said – 'Remember I gave up my chance of being happy to stay with your father and give you the best chance to be happy. When you're unhappy, you let me down.'

Lesley is successful. She loves her work. But in her mid thirties she has not altogether come to terms with her sexuality. She sleeps with many men on a one-night-stand basis:

'I don't want sex to get in the way of making a go of the company. I like it this way, without strings. And the only new men I meet are other women's husbands, so I do less harm this way.'

An Unfair Fate

If motivation did not come from the mother, today's successful women – at least, those over thirty – seem to have had to invent their own. Without conscious anger at some barrier (real or imagined) imposed on them by an unfair fate, or society, or the masculine system, many women might not have felt compelled to break free of society's perception of the female role.

Thus Ellen, who is Irish and took her first job in England as a graduate management trainee, says:

'I actually feel it's a great advantage not to be English in England. If you're from outside, they don't mind if you succeed. They don't seem to think it's at their expense. But what they really don't like is when one of their own does well and becomes successful. Then they do everything they can to cut them down to size – particularly a woman.'

The essential anger vital to the drive to succeed arose in some cases from being written off in some way in childhood. Joan, for instance, was dyslexic:

'That's the key to me. I left school when I was fifteen. I didn't know till I was living in America, only a few years ago. I was hopeless at school, except in Maths, where I came top. I always associated being intelligent with words, and I was driven by the feeling that I was stupid. I had to prove I wasn't.

'Part of ambition for me was helping others. I responded to need. I got a job working for an inner-city housing trust, and it was there I realised I was a natural manager – or rather, an entrepreneur rather than a manager. It was necessary for me to have a good deputy. I produced the flair and resolved problems by the use of ideas.'

Or take Sarah, whose retail group has a turnover of £190 million a year:

'I had two older brothers who were academically clever. Not me. I got Art O level, that's all. I failed Scripture three times, and my father was a clergyman. I never, ever thought of myself as thick. I was hopeless at everything – sport, needlework, everything. I was not a born leader. I went to work on the cosmetic counter of the local department store. I expected to get married and be procreating quite quickly. I used to wonder why I had to keep working for a living this way.

'There was a great social life in the store. I got into a training scheme – no major motivation ... Suddenly I found I was quick with figures, which no one had expected. After that, it was a question of proving that I wasn't a hopeless case. Not long ago, I met an ex-boss who'd thought I was an idiot, and he said, "I was wrong about you, wasn't I?"

'What it's all left me with is a tendency to think it's my fault if people criticise me. When I was made chief executive, my reaction was to say I couldn't do it because I felt too ignorant about financial things and the City. But of course, what's the use of doing something unless you're learning new things?'

Sources of Energy

It is important to try to understand what made successful women want to succeed, because that is the key to their vision of what success enables them to do.

In 1985, a study by the social psychologist Yvan Bordelieu of a number of working women showed that work values for women were related to the personnel management style the subjects would have advocated if they had been in a management position.

Dounne, producer of Gramma's sauces, points out that bringing up her family as a divorced mother taught her to take all the responsibility involved in running a business:

'The difference is that you have to start taking care of yourself as well as other people. That's something you have to learn – and the reality is you never stop learning. Women may have emulated men because they only saw men in controlling positions, but once we can show that we have natural management talent which has been restricted by tradition to our domestic role, we can, if we keep our femininity, bring balance to the business world. At the moment this is made more difficult for us because men have always been aware of women's ability, and now it's emerging into the workplace, they're edgy and scared of our abilities.'

The American social psychologist Carol Gilligan says that though women in our society do the emotional work, both for themselves and for others, though they know they are responsible for feeling, men for doing, women haven't yet recognised that the ability to feel and experience emotion directly is a source of power to change social conditions.

If they haven't actually articulated this source of power,

senior women in management are certainly using it in the performance of their jobs. Their overriding objective is to create a business environment which works – and that means it works for the community or group, not just for them. Karen, the West Midlands headteacher who describes herself as a school manager, says:

'I like organising. I'm a systems kind of person. What I like is being in a position to bring out the best in other people, as opposed to forcing my view on them.'

Sheila, the finance director, also acknowledges that she is motivated by the satisfaction of making a situation work for other people:

'I want to try to make situations better, companies better, for the people in them – and to have the ability to do it, through my position. I see my aim as the good of people as a whole. Some ego does come into it, but I work on the principle that I'm part of a team. I wouldn't be in this position if I didn't want my thoughts to have sway if at all possible, but ultimately I'm looking for the best decision. The best way forward is to work with a team of people who are good and get the best team you can around you.'

And Sarah, the retail chain chief executive, explains what is involved in the fulfilment she gets from making a team work:

'I like being a boss. I'm not bossy, but I like working with a team of young people you can promote. I really want them to succeed. And I'm a very good picker.'

A vision of management as enabling others to create a strong and fulfilled community of workers can force even very successful women to put the good of the company above their own personal interests. Sally says:

'I was a strong leader even from school, but I led by being popular. As a boss, I feel a need for affiliation. It pleases me to please others. Used to excess, this can be a terrible weakness because it can make you unsure and make people distrustful of you as a manager. It means you can agree with everybody else. You hold your own views back, and canvass other people's opinions all the time.

'I was brought up as a very feminine individual. If you think what that actually means – soft-spoken, demure, polite, considerate – that kind of outward behaviour gets a response and strengthens itself because people respond to you as that, so you constantly tend to be it. So people are protective towards you and domineering towards you.

'Sometimes I had to act out of character to seem to be tough enough to have my ambitions recognised. That's one of the hardest things. Even as someone who first wanted to be an actress, it was a hard part to play – it was real and the feelings were real. What made such acting out of character worthwhile, though painful, was that it achieved the best result for me and for others. We achieved an altruistic culture.

'In my first real management role, I had another woman working for me. She was delightful and we were good drinking partners, but she was almost incompetent in certain things. She made mistakes and covered them up. My natural instinct was to help, to say give it to me, I'll do it, and we'll sort it out together. So I was sorting it out and sweeping up after her with my little dustpan and brush. Then my boss – also a woman – coached me. What were the consequences? I was run off my feet, she was driving me mad, and not learning. What are you going to do? Tackle it. So I did, head on. This is what's happened, what are we going to do? We sorted it out the best way it could be done. I felt a tremendous sense of reward, that we had both gained from it.'

Making Things Work

Edith Cresson, as Prime Minister of France involved in a rare senior management role, believes women will give professional efficiency priority over their own personal interests:

'They do this perhaps because it is not always the idea of success which motivates them. What women like is to do something well, to construct something which works, whether it be in industry, in administration, in politics, or wherever. They love whatever runs well.'

This is echoed by Lisa, explaining what she most enjoys about her job as director of an advertising agency:

'It's making a profitable business, seeing things work, the effect advertising has on the way things are made and done, and how it can make people money. I'm very interested in the whole process of business in that sense.'

And Janet, whose entire staff from the subsidiary of a multinational corporation where she was managing director followed her when she left to set up her own company, says:

'I knew I could run a company better than they were doing it. When I started, market research was a craft industry, not a business. They were so inept – they didn't cost jobs properly; they didn't find out what the client's needs were; they were hopelessly overstaffed. I wasn't looking for more money, and responsibility was secondary. What I wanted was more elbow room to do my own thing than I was ever going to get in a company with a Bible as to how things should be carried out.'

When they talk about making things run well, women mean getting the best out of people, and encouraging teamwork, rather than anything mechanical. Professionalism as the best way to make things work in that sense precludes the kind of self-interest attributed to men. Successful women perceive their male colleagues – in meetings, say – as seeing self-interest as an end in itself. Women, after generations of having to rely on outside authority, tend even as bosses to understand what people want *from* them, so even very ambitious women see ego as incorporating us as well as me. Joan, for example, describes what motivated her to start her own company:

'I believe that women at work are interdependent, not independent. My concept of success and fulfilment has to do with what *we* do. I do no favours to other women by curtailing my own fulfilment. Look at any structure where they bring someone up for any reason except ability, and you find it's weakened.'

What Success Means

Making a business situation work gives an ambitious woman proof of her ability to control her own life, to make her own choices. This is an important end-product of women's drive for success in management.

Valerie describes how this has become more important as her career path changed from the initial struggle for seniority to confident achievement as a top manager:

'Success means something different to every woman. To me, it has changed meaning over ten years. It used to mean being on a main board, a flash car, share options, salary, and so on. Now it seems much more having control over my own destiny. It still means a flash car and salary, but that's tempered now by other things in life which are important. It was more status, now it's more to do with power over my own life.'

Andrea, who started her own business and has not worked her way up a corporate ladder, says:

'People say it's very destructive to want to control everything, but another side of it is very constructive. If you're not in control, and don't understand what's happening, you can't really feel confident that you can manage your life. That's what it all boils down to.'

Confidence

Confidence is *the* key factor for every woman in management. If you have the confidence to want to realise your own vision of management, you seek the authority to do so.

Generally speaking, women allowed themselves to become professionally self-confident only once the male system was finally crumbling. Women are often motivated to succeed because they see that something is wrong and want to find a way to put it right. If a system does work, they do not relish change for the sake of it, or to gain personal kudos. Julie, director of a subsidiary of a former nationalised industry, says:

'In lower-graded jobs I felt frustrated because the decisions I was taking weren't the ones I wanted to be taking. I had to make them within a hopeless bureaucratic system which was inept. I thought even my own decisions were wrong in this context, and I wanted to be in a position where I was taking the formative, not the consequential, decisions. That was a large part of my reasons for pushing forward. Now that we have put a much more flexible management system in place, although I want to see my efforts continued, I want to leave and do something else.'

Again, there's a generational aspect. Older women seem to develop confidence from being part of a system that works. For management consultant Lorraine – just thirty – confidence is a technique you acquire. For her, it is automatic once you learn how. Why not? She has no doubts about herself, nor about her assumption that she has a right to be confident. If she makes a mistake, she makes a mistake. She does not have to feel that she has let down the cause of countless other women who would be encouraged by her success. Her attitude contrasts with that of fifty-ish Joan:

'I started out apologising for everything because I thought everyone was so much better than me. I felt I was there under false pretences all the time. I very definitely feel that I'm judged not just on how I manage, but as a sort of test case for other women. I think perhaps I need to feel that. I can do things on behalf of other women I could never do just for my own sake.'

Janet, in her fifties, and head of her own company, believes that young women now come with built-in confidence:

'My confidence when I started in the 1960s was very fragile. As a woman, no one took me seriously. As a manager, I had terrible problems putting over what I wanted. I'd never had to make presentations, and I was thrown into pitching for new business. I was tongue-tied. I couldn't sell myself. My reaction to formally exposing myself was to be deadly serious. It has taken me twenty-five years not to hide behind scientific mishmash, and to make jokes. I was very, very boring. But gradually you gain confidence by being able to do things you doubt you can.

'But the young don't doubt themselves. Young women have outstripped men in confidence, and I wonder where they get it. They're very direct, and there's no kowtowing to age or experience. I suppose actually they see both age and experience as irrelevant in the business world today. It has changed since my day – for instance, anyone with the ability has access to top management now.

'Young women don't hesitate to ask for what they want. You say at assessments, "You've done these things wrong, now what can I do to help you?" and they tell you – you don't allow them enough rope or elbow room; they demand to have their own rights, and to organise their own work. They're very aware of the need for self-development – they've got to go out and do it. They want recognition and money, and they believe in their right to get them.'

One explanation for the increased confidence of young women managers may be that they do actually have statutory as well as ideological rights. Where an older generation of women felt – and were made to feel – that they were working on sufferance, and gained promotion as part of male tokenism, young women are very aware of their rights. Sheila, finance director, says:

'Young women are more aware of their employment rights today. They're not exactly getting litigious, just more aware, and more prepared to use them. If they feel held back, they go to the personnel director and say so. There's an implicit threat of legal action which is not available to men. Also, statistically speaking, their parents were probably divorced at least once, so they've been brought up not to expect a man ever to look after them. They must use what pressure they can.'

Happiness is . . .

There is more involved in job satisfaction than the ability to control systems and lives. Anne, who has given up a senior management position to freelance while her baby is young, is concerned about money, but this is not what she misses most about work:

'The aspect of management I enjoyed was doing something you get a kick out of, and have a feeling for. That involved all kinds of moral and political satisfaction. I have friends who moved from social work when the do-gooding part of their make-up got weakened by impotence. They turned to the business world, where they were able to satisfy their moral side and feel they were achieving at the same time.

'I also miss the social context of work – being part of a team with other people. Even when at a few stages I've been finding the job itself worthless and uninteresting, what kept it going was the people – not just seeing them, but the whole sense of community involved. There have been phases when relationships at work have been much more stimulating than outside social relationships.'

These are not women who see the pursuit of happiness as something unprofessional or selfish. Overwhelmingly, they enjoy their work when it enables them to be part of a happy community. In many cases, the traditional 'feminine' ethic has moved beyond the domestic arena and into the workplace.

All successful women enjoy their work. It is probably the central source of both pleasure and satisfaction in their lives. Not one of those interviewed who is married would willingly give up her job to accommodate a husband's career move. Those with children had all decided to have them only when they felt they had reached a level of seniority and confidence in their abilities where having a baby was not a threat to their careers.

Those who assume that women always put others' interests before their own may be frightened by the toughness and clarity of such women. But how much is envy involved here? There's a feeling, though few would admit to it, that such a level of fulfilment should demand a price. Psychologically? Not according to Donald Klein, Professor of Psychiatry at Columbia University. He points out that work plays an important part in preventing demoralisation because it gives a person evidence that she can be effective.

Lesley, who runs her own television production company, says that for her, work success is an addiction:

'I sometimes think being around me in my private life must be like living with a junkie. But for me it's better than any drug. The stress used to upset me sometimes, before I had the confidence in myself to know I could cope with a situation as it arose. Now it gets the adrenalin going, because something that asks questions of my ability to cope is a challenge, and that's what working is all about – resolving problems. I don't just have the delusion I can fly. I know I can.'

'My God,' said a male friend who brought in coffee while I was talking to her, and heard what Lesley said, 'she may be female, but is she really a woman?'

A New Identity

My friend's reaction is not so outlandish, after all. Academic studies of working women have tended to concentrate on how they fit paid work into their primary function as wives and mothers. Inevitably, the resulting image of working women is of put-upon female victims. Society has accepted without question the theory that a man promotes his individuality and independence through work. The hierarchical structure is designed to allow him to do so, through competition and conflict, with winners trampling losers on the way to the top. Male identity thus depends on separation from other people. So independence equals maturity, and masculine maturity is achieved by learning in childhood to reject the emotional, loving, sharing feminine.

Despite tremendous social changes, many people continue to define woman's development, on the other hand, in terms of the qualities demanded of her by her role as daughter, wife and mother. Her identity is not separate, it is contingent on other people. This meant, for older ambitious women at work, that they tended to confuse success with winning the approval of the people they work with.

Sarah, retail chain chief executive, admits that even five years ago, when she was a senior manager, she found herself falling automatically into the role of the helpless little woman in the face of even the mildest confrontation. It was impossible, she says, for her to take an adult decision and say exactly what she wanted done:

'I used to be very useless at saying yes or no. Whatever my title, I couldn't escape from this feeling that I must be wrong because I'm only the little woman. I'd say, "I take your point", and try to persuade them. You sound very foolish if you're constantly agreeing with somebody and then talking him out of it because it was a stupid idea in the first place. But don't a lot of women do that – play along that they're dim-witted and persuade people to do what they want to humour them?'

Fear of Flying

American psychologist Marina Horner has pointed out that men and women in management are motivated by the hope for success and the fear of failure. But women also fear success – because of the conflict between their upbringing and their drive to achieve.

One way women cope with this is to put the onus on some outside force – an unfair fate, or male attitudes. It's almost as though some women try to handicap themselves before they start so that if they do succeed, they can't be 'blamed' by other women for setting themselves apart from them.

Dounne describes how this affects black women:

'Black women trying to achieve our own levels have been undermined and undervalued for so long we've reached the point where we undervalue ourselves. We are undervalued as women, and we are undervalued as black. We run the risk constantly of being placed in the category of special needs, which keeps you in a perpetual state of deprivation. In reality we have natural talent which has remained dormant because we have been trained and redirected from school into a certain view of our lives. It isn't deliberate undermining. It's tradition.'

Management consultant Lorraine mentions women's tendency to 'place themselves in the category of special needs' in connection with a colleague who is about five years younger:

'She's always coming in and sitting down all white-faced and miserable, asking how I cope. I've heard it so often, and I usually give her some bracing advice. But one day I'd had enough. She says she's hopeless, but she got a degree from Oxford. She goes on about how awful her husband is, but actually she's behaving like a doormat and blaming him for not telling her not to. She spends all this time agonising and falls behind with her work because of personal reasons she's creating for herself. What she wants is an alibi for failure. And the silly thing is, if she wasn't looking for that, she wouldn't be failing.'

Valerie, too, is impatient with the self-inflicted victim syndrome:

'When I was first promoted, there was no executive loo for women. I said I'd go down to the floor below and use the lavatory in the general office. The board – all men – were scandalised that I'd have to walk through the general office, so everyone would know where I was going. I thought it gave me the opportunity to pick up on what was going on, but there was real concern that I should have to mix like that.

'They were giving me the chance to be a victim. We can all be victims if we want. We can say the system doesn't allow us; there's a glass ceiling. It won't get us anywhere. The fundamental difference between men and women in management is that if men see an obstacle they automatically look for a way round, whereas women have an excuse to fall back on if they want – "My way was blocked." That's very easy to do. It's an alibi for failure.'

3

POWER:
THE GOOD, THE BAD & THE UGLY

Power: Status

Traditionally, women have not had power in the work-place. Power behind the throne? That boils down to influence, which is quite a different thing. It depends entirely for effect on reference to someone else's power. Generally speaking, women have tended to be overlooked when it comes to handing out power. The very concept flouted the basis of definitions of 'feminine'. A woman might benefit from the power of a man close to her, even partake of some of his authority in the sense of 'do to her as you would be done to by him'. But without access to the ingredients of power – money, status, knowledge – a woman could not claim any of her own.

Even when women achieved one or some of the ingredients of power through work, they tended not to seek it. Mostly they huddled in subservient positions as secretaries and clerks and various kinds of assistant. But even the very few women who climbed the executive ladder to power-bearing positions were likely to find it suspect. To enjoy power was to draw too deep a demarcation between themselves and the rest of their sex.

Men automatically take power from their status. This does not seem to work as easily for women. Even very senior female managers have to persuade themselves they have the *right* to power. For them, the automatic authority that comes from status is not enough. It takes more than that for a woman to convince herself and others of real power behind seniority. That is something women can achieve only individually for themselves. Karen has experience of this at group meetings of headteachers:

'Men just assume they can take charge. Their position as heads gives them delusions of power, and that's all the authority they need. What annoys me is that women of equal status and seniority let them do it. They see their jobs as being licensed by men, and they even dress up as though they were on show. I even tried to set up a Women in Management group among West Midlands teachers, but they think it's all left-wing rubbish.'

And Valerie finds that though members of her staff accept that she has power over them because of her status, it's not enough to convince her:

'I overheard a conversation here. Someone said, "Don't let Valerie hear, she'll be really annoyed." I asked about this, and my secretary said, "Well, you never lose your temper, Valerie, but none of us would ever cross you." "Why?" "We just wouldn't." I find it amusing because I'm actually a very even-tempered person, but there's this perception – because of the position I'm in, I suppose – that it wouldn't be wise to cross me. There was a time when some of my work was lost. I said I'd got the notes and I'd do it again. *They* made a fuss. My secretary came and said they felt really bad, and actually if I'd shout, they'd feel a bit better. I said that meant they could all decide I'm a miserable cow and they don't have to feel guilty any more. She said that was right.

'I suppose partly they don't want to lose my respect – that's what I think power has to be based on, mutual respect.'

As more women went into the workforce, most at a menial level, it became fashionable for companies to promote a few token women. Tokenism offers status without power. Today, though, a new generation of successful young women has established power as a platform of reconstructed womanhood. Chief executive Sarah says:

'I've reached the point now where my seniority gives me security. I could be sacked tomorrow and I'd still know that I am successful. No one can take that away from me now.'

Women's Power Outside the Workforce

Women who are now coming to terms with their right to exercise power within the business system have had to change an ingrained perception outside the workforce of where women's power lies.

Once, women's power was centred on their reproductive power. This, though, has lost much of its political influence. Since the Pill and the 1967 Abortion Act, women have demonstrated strongly that they do not want their security to depend on their reproductive power. The birth rate fell from over one million in 1965 to 675,000 in 1974. It has remained roughly at that level. The 'important' women are no longer just wives and mothers but those who work, the independent ones, and – particularly as change-agents – the successful working ones.

Then again, as management consultant Lorraine says:

'Women used to be powerful role models in the female ghettoes like voluntary work, where they were allowed to sublimate their desire for work outside the home. But because they were role models to women who were unable or unwilling to take on the mainstream, they had no broader impact.'

Also, the ambitious women who were trying to make their work important enough to attract power had to contend with the jealousy of the powerful men's wives whose own interests were served by preserving the male-dominated status quo which gave them security. Ellen describes what happens:

'When I have to assert my authority over a meeting of senior male managers, I find men often take their views of women from their wives and their friends, who are not women who work. Men use examples like these in a very powerful way. They counter me by saying, "That's not my experience."'

In a previous senior management job, Lorraine found that men committed to encouraging and promoting women to senior positions pandered to their wives' and other women's potential hostility to a female high-flier:

'I feel I suffered from the prejudice of women who did not understand that the power game in business can't be judged by outside criteria. I had two senior mentors in the company. Cross-sex mentoring is very difficult because of the innuendoes. In both cases it was misinterpreted and the guys were very embarrassed. They wouldn't have lunch openly with me, which they did with male colleagues. If they did have lunch with me, it was in a clandestine manner in the corner of some dark restaurant. Of course that made it look as though there was something to hide.'

Joan believes that her fortysomething contemporaries who were ambitious, even though few of them were successful careerists, began to exert power on business management while still conforming to the traditional dependent conventions of womanhood:

'Women of my age – nearly fifty – went out and changed the schools. When I took my children to primary school, parents were not allowed beyond a certain point. Well, we forced our way into the schools, with PTAs and fund-raising. We've been followed by a quite different group of mothers, very tough, powerful women coming in and changing things, so the mothers are now in charge. What they say counts.'

The Old: The Young

Joan goes on to say:

'Older women think they have to apologise for power. They behave as though they've got where they are by default, or luck, not on their own merit. If they're apologising for having power, they're more or less making it useless.'

Finance director Sheila, at thirty-seven, feels that she straddles a generational change:

'The previous generation seemed to feel they didn't have a right to power, though they wanted it. Something built-in made them apologise. They felt they had to be grateful. Women a little younger than I am now take it as a right, as something they earn.'

Inevitably, as they grew out of their submissive domestic supporting role, women came up against aspects of power that were new to them. Generally, because they saw power as a male province, they tended to talk about their relationship to it in terms of powerlessness. This is not so different from the premiss behind trade unions – that workers seeking higher wages and better conditions were powerless as individuals, but strong as a united brotherhood. But, unlike the brothers, ambitious women who sought power disrupted their relationships with women as a whole. Femininity decreed that they were self-serving and selfish. In consequence, unlike men in the unions, women have had few or no female leaders.

Even today, older women who do have power often still conceal it, presenting themselves as dogsbodies overwhelmed with work to elicit sympathy and disguise their authority. Their approach is to demonstrate that their power is actually a surfeit of the feminine norm of being put-upon. Personnel manager Suzanne describes a former colleague:

'She was the only woman in senior management, and she just took everything on. She made herself seem indispensable to the men at the top. She was always feeling ill, sending us out for pills and prescriptions, and putting on a brave face making everyone feel guilty because she had so much work to do. The funny thing is, she moved to work in an all-women office, and someone I met later said that there they all thought she was a lazy cow.'

Powerless women can exert considerable unconscious pressure on their ambitious sisters to maintain their connection with a female norm which rejects the 'selfishness' of the individual striving necessary to gain power. School manager Karen describes how her junior colleagues do this:

'I find junior colleagues compete with me for my time. They come to me with problems we both know they can sort out, but they'll risk me thinking less of them as teachers just so that they can make me spend the time on them. The idea is that the more time I spend with them, the less I'll have to spend on my own job, which involves having power over them. I do feel that they're trying to make me one of them, rather than a boss. It can be beguiling, too, because I want to use the power I have to create a team of equals – but the trouble is, I can't achieve the team of equals without the power to impose it and replace the old male autocratic system.'

Dealing with Male Power

The corporate arena is still overwhelmingly male-dominated, and ambitious women have to assert their authority in this context. This can go against the female grain. Suzanne says:

'I have trouble asserting myself with women. It's not because I think assertiveness is a form of collusion with the male system, but I believe real change for the better in the business culture doesn't mean special treatment for women, but treating everyone the same. There are still a lot of women who don't know how to deal with that. They expect what I can only call emotional concessions. But if you play that game, you're right back where you started from, with women as the victims.'

When successful women in business say they 'played the male game', they always describe it as taking aggressive action, which they did deliberately, aware that they were putting on an act. But that is not quite the same as saying they are acting out of character. Janet, as chief executive, remembers a clash with Brian, her managing director and partner:

'We have always been at one on any major issue until last year, when he couldn't see how destructive a particular person was. I played the masculine game (which I don't like doing) by not trying to change his mind or compromising, but taking it to the board and pulling rank. I didn't like doing it, but it was essential. Afterwards he respected me for doing it – but he didn't expect I would do it. If you play the masculine game hard, they accept it. It's more comprehensible to them than the oblique way.'

Karen, whose management style as head of a school often leads her to use soft words in deference to a general paranoia among class teachers which she well understands from her own teaching days, also felt forced to play the male game:

71

'A male teacher did something I saw as totally unprofessional. I called him in and bawled him out – and threatened him. He thought I was so angry I lost my temper – but I didn't. I sat and thought about it and did it on purpose. I felt I should frighten him, although that's the opposite to the way I see good management. Being a boss is to give people confidence.

'Equally, I have a woman teacher who is overmaternal in managing her class. She teaches the youngest classes, and she let the children sit on her knee. She manhandled them, too – taking them by the arm and putting them where she wanted them to be, not telling them to go there. It's to do with the maternal attitude to being a teacher, making the children dependent on her. It's not professional. She tried to draw my sting by being maternal to me, too. She had the attitude that because I was female, I'd need a shoulder to cry on.'

Some powerful women are unwilling to lose the influence women have always exercised over men – it can make power seem less of a confrontation between male and female. One of the former staff of the now defunct news magazine *Now* described what happened at the wake held in the office after the last issue was printed:

'A lot of people were very depressed and unhappy. And then an extraordinary thing happened: some of the women took male colleagues away from the party into the individual offices. The women were just as redundant as the men. The jobs were just as important to most of them. But this sort of tacit thing swept over everyone, and it was accepted that these women provided comfort and solace. It wasn't anything that came from the men.

It was almost as though the women couldn't do anything else.'

Anne, aged thirty-nine, admits that in her first job in management she quite deliberately set out to 'mother' her boss to allay his suspicions:

'This man had problems about women at work. He thought their place was in the home. The way I played it, a mixture of maternal instincts and child instincts went into mothering him. Certainly I'd affect a concern or curiosity about him and about his home life, and I'd sit and listen while he talked, bored rigid by what he was saying, but I wouldn't stop him. Like a therapist, I let him carry on. If you equate mothering with sub-mission – which I do, in parts – then I used that submiss-ive element on my boss. It involves lessening your demands for someone else's benefit. I never did that with peers or with women – though I was very supportive and sympathetic with secretaries.'

Learning Power: Mentors

Many ambitious women learned how to gain power – and how to exercise it – from mentors. Successful managers are not born, they are made. Mentors, in nearly every case, played an important part in making them what they are today. And of course, because until recently there were so few women in top management, this mentor was almost always a man. Lorraine sees this as an established part of the system:

'People get to the top by having mentors. It's usually man to man. What the senior man gets out of it is

73

information. At the top of an organisation you can never learn what's going on underneath, what the troops feel. And the older person basks in reflected glory if the younger is attractive. There's nothing sexual in that.'

An ambitious woman's mentor is more a father figure than a sex symbol. Recruitment agency director Valerie, for example, used hers to initiate her into the male business culture, much as women take their connection with traditional feminine culture from their mothers. I mentioned earlier that fathers, however loved and admired, had played very little part in the making of any of these successful women. The mentor fills that cultural gap. Valerie says:

'I had a very good mentor. He didn't mollycoddle me, or treat me any differently to anyone else in the department. The first time I made a cock-up – in a situation with the unions – he didn't say there there, but told me I'd cocked it up, I'd better sort it. I had to apologise to the union guy and get out of it. I learned a very important lesson – that you don't play to win at all costs, you leave yourself a way out. You don't always learn that young. It cost me a lot, but it taught me.'

And Lisa remembers:

'I lacked confidence because I felt I'd just been very lucky in the jobs I'd had. But then I worked with a mentor who inspired me. You can build your confidence on people like that.'

This may be true, but as Sheila adds: 'The trouble is that men want to maintain the system and feed myths about female priorities.' And Suzanne described the mentor relationship as flirtatious, but never erotic: 'If he becomes a lover, it is a different thing.'

Power and the Use of Sex

Men's perception of female priorities is changing, but the system is often still stuck with seeing women primarily as wives, mothers and sex objects – the carers and dependants defined as incapable of achieving adulthood. Their sex is what limits them – and men have always used women's 'inferior' gender status to keep them in their place.

Some women have colluded with this, and used it to manipulate men in their turn. One or two of our older senior women did use their sex to manage the relationship with senior men. Remember the demoted managing director who won her way back to the top job by 'immobilising' the man brought in over her: 'The way to conquer him was to have an affair with him. So I did.' Mention sex in connection with women in the business culture and you still get a man saying 'Yes, please'. And many women have to stop themselves automatically adopting the victim position. A radical change of attitude involves some pretty deep-rooted prejudice on both sides. Sex is a subject fraught with emotional overtones on which men and women are deeply divided by upbringing, expectations, and even understanding of each other's basic terms of reference.

But there are signs of change. Some ambitious and successful women are now beginning to turn erstwhile negative aspects of being female to positive and even aggressive use against male sexual exploitation at work.

Janet, who founded her own market research company and now heads the international set-up formed after a merger, mentioned earlier that the young women who work for her are very well aware of their rights, and use them as an unspoken threat. This applies to sex as well as equal opportunity. Consider this quotation from a woman complaining that she is the victim of sexual harassment. She was quoted in a national newspaper as the victim of unwanted sexual advances from a former boss:

'He was a married man who promised me a nice career and quick salary increases if only I would accept his friendship. He kept hinting that my post and my future depended on him, so I began accepting lunch dates. In the end, although he was not my type of man, I gave in. We had an affair which lasted three years, until I finally realised he would never leave his wife.'

This woman is prepared to use sex to obtain power. He, presumably, feels that no defence is needed; she pleads that she is the victim. Traditional definitions of womanhood allow women to assert themselves primarily only through their victimhood – a form of appeasement, a way of neutralising envy or enmity, along the lines of 'I don't know how you keep your house so clean, mine's always filthy'.

One or two of my older senior women felt that they had needed to use their sexuality to manage their working relationship with senior male colleagues. This can range from a manipulative affair to 'aggravated flirtation'.

Personnel director Suzanne watched a young female colleague use her sexual power very effectively:

'She was very pretty, blonde, with a good figure. She was very ambitious. I was senior to her, and at one time she thought I might be useful to her. She tried coming to me as an older, wiser woman asking my advice – not for direct help, you understand, but for encouragement and guidance. She tried to get a rise out of my maternal feelings, but I'm not very maternal and I resented her approaching me on that level. I was also actually surprised at how incompetent she was. It was amazing she'd got where she was, really.

'But then I saw how she set about senior men. Most of them are really very unsophisticated on any but a strict business level. They didn't know what hit them. She was a real prick-tease. They fell for the whole thing, and then she'd pull the "Oh, if only I weren't married we could consummate our great love. Perhaps there might be a chance of our being alone together if I were your deputy ..." It worked like a charm. She's a main board director where she works now – and still married.'

But for many younger women, these old sexual games have become irrelevant. Janet has noticed this. She is American, though she has lived here for thirty years. She visits the United States on business at least once a year:

'Last year, I noticed something very new at business meetings. There is no flirting. Not a glimmer. At dinner afterwards, I asked what had happened. The people there agreed it was true. The women said it showed men had stopped seeing them as different – meaning inferior. Power dressing, they said, was the nail in the coffin of flirtation. Women were saying, "You can't treat me this way because now I've got to look just like you."'

In the UK, according to Clare, who is a senior personnel manager in the pub trade:

'There is still flirtation at senior management meetings where there are very few women. But it's done with more caution, because from a man it can very easily go into sexual harassment.'

Men's sexual authority has lost much of its potency as a means of control. According to Valerie:

'Young women in senior positions don't recognise what lies behind men's use of sex. They don't see a problem where older women do. Younger women expect to be treated on an equal basis, and they will make it very clear they're not happy if they're not.

'But with senior older men, it's the only way they know how to approach senior women. It's going to be very difficult for older men coming to terms with working for young women. I've seen examples where the young female executive is totally intolerant. She dismisses him, doesn't empathise or understand. Invariably he tries to flirt because that's all he understands.'

As they feel that their most powerful means of control over women at work is declining, men seem at a loss. Karen describes how a single male member of staff responds to being in a minority among an overwhelming majority of women:

'I know he feels very isolated. The management system I inherited was very male-dominated, and now that I've changed it to a much more open and informal sort of school, he is at a loss. He doesn't understand that as one man among many women he has more power in lots of ways, because of their reactions to him. Their expectations are coded to male authority. The advantage to women in the opposite situation is not, I think, an advantage of power. Manipulation, perhaps, but that's using aspects of femininity to play games, and I object to that – though I may do it sometimes.'

Anger and Power

Women who use their sexuality as part of the power game undermine their female colleagues. They are rejecting professional standards in favour of the old-fashioned male concept of female behaviour, which in the business world has traditionally confirmed women's second-class status. Ellen abominates even banter between men and women at work:

'It's actually one of the most difficult things women have to deal with; it's so marginalising, so degrading, so isolating. When it's on a playful basis it's difficult to deal with, and if it goes further it's sexual harassment, which must be the pits. I am very careful to make my views known in a very loud way which is supportive of other women.'

If, as Janet says, American women have eradicated flirting from business meetings, this is not necessarily a way of disarming male power games, but shows that ambitious women in general are actually beginning to express their anger at the tactics of female colleagues. The involvement of sexuality in the competitive process of the workplace can only obstruct the development of an acceptable framework for women to exercise power.

But anger can be part of the motivation to gain power. That's why it is often difficult for women to assert authority over other women: anger between women is a betrayal of sisterhood. Whatever the source of that anger – discrimination, men, other women, the system – power makes it possible to stand up for oneself. Joan says:

'I was working for a charity, where I ran a department. The bulk of the organisation was a huge bureaucracy, but we were a module of ideas. I was frustrated and angry enough with the bureaucratic side to get aggressive about the creative side of charity. That gave me confidence. And then I also got so angry about the way people we were trying to help made it impossible sometimes for us to give them help, because of their attitude or behaviour. I had to learn to express my anger to them. Once we understood each other, I could exercise my authority.'

Many successful women are wary of making enemies of other women. Their instinct to make friends as self-protection means that it is difficult for them deliberately to risk making an enemy of another woman by getting angry with her. Anne describes the way she believes senior women in management have found to avoid hurting each other:

'I've said I used flirtation to establish a relationship with my male boss. It was a rather submissive way, involving a mixture of control and submission.

'I think there's a sort of flirtation between women, too. Flirtation changes as you get older; it has to do with ideas, discussions, and more growth. It's about shared mental enjoyment in some way. I used to say that I liked working as a team. I think the reason I thought and said that a lot was in order not to appear threatening or to try to justify competitiveness by not putting myself out as an individual but saying I'm willing to subsume myself within a set of working relationships that are non-competitive. Even so, I admit I felt pretty angry about people getting ahead of me. But the only anger I expressed was when I'd blame our boss, who called himself a benevolent dictator and expected us to compete workwise for his favours.'

Power: Women as Role Models

If younger women are marginalising sex as a counter in the power game, this may be because there are now senior women with real authority who have changed the business atmosphere. Male mentors, too, have probably had their day. Older men's experience has less relevance now for highly educated young women entering new-technology industries where men do not have a long tradition of domination to fall back upon. There are now female role models.

There is a significant difference between the image of business projected by well-intentioned male mentors and by female role models. Mentors, who are well established, have inbuilt confidence in their own authority. Janet, in her first management job after leaving America at nineteen, valued what she learned from her boss in her first management job:

'It was an old-established family food business, and he owned it. He was very difficult in many respects. We all had to clock on at 8.30 or we lost 10 per cent of our salary. That applied to everyone, from the managing director down. Then we weren't allowed to take any of the company products out of the building. He hated redheads. One day he fired the same man four times because he had red hair. Department heads moved him to different jobs in the building to try and get round it, but he fired him each time . . .'

From his example Janet learned what she calls 'useful lessons' about the use and abuse of power. Female role models, like Karen, usually lack that kind of arrogance. They are successful women whose experience of management structure and skills is much more relevant today to younger women than anything an older male mentor can offer:

'For one thing, it's a straightforward relationship. Nobody is going to accuse you of sleeping your way to the top when it's a woman boss who gives you a helping hand. When there were very few women at the top to provide role models, they were isolated from junior levels below. Junior women distrusted them, or thought of them as male collaborators. Or senior women thought they thought that. Anyway, senior women didn't get anything back – picking out bright young women would have been as hopeless as backing a lame horse, the odds were so stacked against females. The woman boss couldn't be seen to make such a sentimental and risky management decision.'

Now it's in the interests of senior women to mentor younger ones. They get the same flow of information from below as junior men provide for their older male mentors. Because it's a two-way relationship, it's much more equal.

'Once you take gratitude out of the equation, you've got a genuinely fruitful partnership,' says Lorraine. She accepts that she is herself a role model:

'Younger women are always coming in and asking me how I manage a six-figure-salary job and being a wife and mother. In everything I do, I feel I'm representing other women. If I can't keep ahead of the game, I am aware that would be used as an excuse not to let other women try.'

There are still hangovers from the past which complicate women's acceptance of role-model status. Often senior women who are looked on as role models by younger women achieved their status in a male-dominated system where evaluations of working women were made entirely by men. So these women, haunted by a subconscious feeling that they somehow got where they were by luck or patronage rather than ability, often feel powerless. Fiona, thirty-one, made a director of a small company after some years as a line manager, tells how insecure she felt:

'I'd done very well because I was nice to the men, and I was willing to charm my way through confrontation to get my own way. That was simply the easiest way to do it, and I got results because I was lucky enough to have good advice from the top man. The others didn't get the same chance to talk to him and find out what he thought. But then we were taken over and everything changed. We got a new MD ten years younger than me. He didn't respond to me at all as a woman, though he wasn't unpleasant. I just didn't know how to approach him, and it made me very insecure about the kind of woman I am. I was terrified that my whole success had been based on sex. I didn't know if I'd be able to go about managing on any other basis.'

A woman in this position, even though she is undervaluing herself, has no confidence in her power to support younger women whom she actually sees as a threat. Rather than offer support, she may respond by fighting younger women for what she has actually already won.

Julie, a senior manager in a business which employs a large proportion of women at lower levels, is very well aware that she is a role model for a number of women encouraged by her example – and by extended selection systems she has been instrumental in bringing in – to break into management. But she feels threatened by the role, even fraudulent:

'I know other women are encouraged by my example. I get great fulfilment from giving other people opportunities to grow. But I've applied for voluntary redundancy because I find a personal conflict. I don't feel comfortable in my management role – the constraints of it, the long hours, not having space to myself to do other things I want to do, the feeling that though I'm interested in my job, it consumes too much of my life. I feel the role is now forcing me out of character. Achieving a new atmosphere of opportunity for women in a very male hierarchical system has given me great satisfaction, but I don't want other women to think I'm endorsing the system. But I'm prepared to take a drop in income now to escape from the constant discomfort of being miserable because of the mismatch between the job and the real me.'

Karen – who, in the current education system, describes herself as the managing director of a school rather than a headteacher – found that she had to create herself as a role model to achieve the kind of leadership which suits her management aims. But she is more at ease with the management persona she exemplifies than she used to be as a teacher under masculine-style management:

'I took over with a new female deputy, so the management of the school went from all-male to all-female. Otherwise the staff was the same – just two men teachers, the rest women. I was younger than any of them.

'In the immediate aftermath of the male management, the staff looked on me as an alien being. They expected me to know more than I may know. There was an element of being a superperson – nothing to do with being a woman. I refused to be called headmistress. I'm the head. If letters arrived addressed to Mr, or Dear Sir, I sent them back. I get annoyed by the refusal to admit the possibility of a female manager.

'The staff had certain expectations about my role. They didn't expect me to be friendly. I insisted on being called Karen from day one, even by the caretaker. My management style is not dictatorial in any way. I did set out to change the style of management at the school.

'My vision for the school was for a team of professionals on equal terms. The fact that I do the job I do doesn't mean it's not equal. It's not better, just different. The idea was to lead by example.

'At first, the staff couldn't cope. For instance, I'd come into a staff meeting not understanding why they wouldn't speak. My deputy told me they weren't allowed to speak in staff meetings which were held to give them information. If they argued, they were put down.

'My jobs as manager and role model were part and parcel of the same thing. I couldn't make my style of management work without becoming a role model to show that it can work – and that if I can do it, so can they. I can't think of a single member of my staff who doesn't have a self-esteem problem, including me. Actually, I don't think that's a bad thing. Totally self-confident people are never going to be able to reflect on their own work and improve. Maybe you need a small corner that says "that's not good enough". It's a big issue with women – it's what pushes them on. You set yourself unrealistic targets when there's a problem. If you can draw back the targets to make them realistic – through experience, I suppose – you're going to be a better manager.'

According to Gillian Shephard, all the senior and successful women she invited to breakfast sessions at her office to brief her on the state of business play wanted to see the image of business changed to encourage more women to go into it. They felt that simply trying to explain what it's like to run your own business was not enough: they had to project the possibilities, get some glamour into the image. And they recognise that they themselves are the medium for the message.

What they offer is more developmental. Their ambivalence about their function as role models is often due to lack of confidence in their own authority. Ellen, personnel director, says:

'I'm not sure how far I feel I'm constantly on the line is because I'm a woman or because I'm involved in training. There's a feeling they can both be done without. It adds to the non-positive pressure that both I and my profession are on trial. The managing director has actually said that now if he had two equal candidates he'd go for the woman because he'd know that to get where she was she'd have had to work harder. That is true of me. But if a woman blots her copybook, it can affect the prospects of many other women. Men aren't held responsible for each other's success like that.'

This often leads to a situation where the woman who knows she is a role model because she is successful feels pulled two ways – between her own interests and those of aspiring women to whom she feels responsible. This is Sarah's problem:

'I'm not comfortable with my public persona. It's so cruel to put people on pinnacles and then shoot them down. My situation in the company lays me open to this, but it is only making me a sacrificial lamb. Being a role model is doing the job well, it's not moaning about sexual harassment and the glass ceiling. I have to play the part of Sarah, business-woman, to the extent that if I go out on a date, I can't shed it. The top-woman persona is a bit of a tyrant. I don't mind being a role model as long as women don't try to make themselves into something they're not. I've got a girlfriend who tried to superimpose what she thought I was on to herself, and it was quite wrong for her. It's quite dangerous on a personal level – especially if what somebody thinks you are is a persona you have to assume as part of the business image, not the real you at all!'

Seizing Authority

In terms of male concepts of power – that it stems from conflict, aggression, victory, self-assertion – there is still unease in the way some women wear it. Julie says:

'I don't enjoy chairing a meeting if it's on a contentious issue. If I've got to negotiate with the unions, and there's a situation of conflict, I find it hard to handle. I don't like doing it. I prefer a situation where things are informal, and that's not always possible. When I was at lower grades I saw taking decisions as exercising power, and I wanted to be in a position to take them myself, but I find where there's a balance of views I sometimes find decisions hard.

It's hard to see the best way to go. I've been accused of railroading, and if I've made up my mind I won't take opposing views into account. Sometimes I feel I'm over-forceful at meetings where I'm the only woman in order to get listened to. I overstress something unimportant. I think basically I probably lack confidence in my own authority.'

Sarah, on the other hand, says:

'I let people get on with their own jobs, but I never delegate responsibility. On good days, it's interest, on bad ones, interference. I'm very hands-on. I don't do anything, but I want to know everything. I've a great capacity for remembering things – both business, and personal things about workers.

'I don't think managers have the right to think they can do what they want to do. They ought to do what company policy is, so I lead from the top. If they don't like it, I've enough confidence in myself to say that's how to do it. Five years ago I'd have said I took their point and tried to persuade them. I used to be very useless at saying yes or no. I'm now confident enough to say do this. If I avoided using my power, no one would know where they were. I want us all to work in a happy company, and I think power gives me the ability to help make it that way.'

Fifteen years ago, social psychologist Marsha Jacobsen and others published research into women as authority figures. It is interesting because it gives an insight into the way women without access to female power perceive it. As part of the experiment, they got men and women to read aloud accounts of different situations where an authority figure confronts a subordinate who has done something wrong. Then they evaluated the authority figure.

In the first examples, the authority figures took a hard line with their subordinates. Judgement was most negative where a female authority figure was tough on a male subordinate. In the second examples, authority figures were lenient with their subordinates. A female authority figure being lenient with a female subordinate was looked on most negatively.

So, Jacobsen asks, are perceptions of a woman as an authority figure affected by the exertion of, or failure to exert, her authority? She found that exertion of authority is seen as 'male', and a man exerting authority is 'doing his job'. There was special hostility, from both men and women, for the woman who has power and uses it. In practice, though, the sex of the subordinate on the receiving end makes a difference. If she is a woman, bawled out by a woman, only a partial reversal of roles is involved; whereas if it's a man, there is a turnabout of traditional roles. The experiment suggested that the reaction to a woman in a position of authority is determined not by her actions, but by the sex of the person she exerts power over. There is a feeling that a man in a subordinate position isn't deliberately subordinate, but a woman in authority does deliberately seek power.

Incidentally, the experiment also showed that hostility to a woman who has power and uses it does not apply when she is exerting authority over children. Today Karen makes the same distinction in analysing the demands power makes on her as school head rather than class teacher:

'As a class teacher, you do manage when you're in charge of children, but it's easier. You've got power over children, haven't you? *Per se*. The set-up between a teacher and a class of thirty children means they accept the premise that they do what you say. Managing teachers is different. You get all the egos, and their personal problems. Teaching is very personal, and when you're standing in front of a class as a teacher, you're giving not just your knowledge – you're giving them yourself as a person. Any criticism of your teaching is therefore criticism of you as a person. Managing staff is different because of the egos. It's part of my job as head now, but the situation is only just changing, and in the past it was never the job of the head to manage. Before, the head was top dog and expected just to be a curriculum leader.'

Female Authority Now More Acceptable?

Women have gained considerable access to authority in the fifteen years since Jacobsen published her research. How much has changed, then, since she found that women who exert power invite hostility from both men and women?

Things are changing, but perhaps not so much because society has got used to the idea that power is not by definition a male prerogative – I think there is more general hostility to any exertion of power. In society as a whole we have seen power moving away from an exclusively male Establishment. Women have a new authority in the financial sector, and this will be a source of growing influence as broader international fiscal factors marginalise British party politicians in making crucial economic policy. Recent events, too, have weakened the power of the male-dominated judiciary. Once such centres of masculine authority are proved fallible, or cannot be taken seriously, they lose the ability to enforce their power. Now that the male Establishment power bases are desperately trying to claw back their authority, it is worth noting that they are using women to front their attempts to seem trustworthy. Thus in the last year, women have appeared on television to put the Establishment view on the nuclear industry, Soviet defence cuts, City fraud, aviation, the Gulf War, and pollution. Trust is an important ingredient in the successful wielding of power – and in the wake of the male system's persistent betrayal of public trust, it is significant that public power is being built around women.

Is this because female authority has become more acceptable than male? At least women have fewer precedents of abusing power. The bullying style of the 1980s sprang from complacency, and faith in the future. In the 1990s, though, faith in the future is more like an alcoholic's abstinence – an infinite prospect of taking one day at a time. Women's understanding of the nature of power embraces this, where men's does not. Training company managing director Sally says:

'Power means something different to me as a woman from what it involves for men – my husband, for example. Power to him is power over others to be exercised, and to be made as public as possible. He's saying, "If you don't know I'm in charge, then I'm going to tell you." To me, it's something quiet, something I don't have to prove. I can look powerful – clothes and cars mean a lot – but I don't have to rub someone's nose in it. How you exercise power without doing that is in getting results, having the right answers, being respected but not feared. Men quite like to be feared.'

And Ellen, training director:

'I think power means something different to men and women. It involves status for men, and the things they can do. I think it's true of women, too, that they like recognition. But as a woman, I use my position of power to get things done. It gives me great job satisfaction, the enablement side, and the confidence you see grow in people because of what you get done.

'On the training side, women are grateful for what you do, and say thanks. Men need to be reminded that they got where they are through training, and they need to offer it to others. They're very arrogant about it – say they didn't need it. They say three days' training could be done in a day. You have to exert authority obliquely. I say, "With your experience, I'd only expect to need one day, but we're not talking about you." It's flattering in one context, but not really.'

Power and Responsibility

Lisa, too, sees power as a responsibility to others:

'I'm working part-time while my daughter is young. No one else has been able to do this, but I was senior enough to demand it. Now other women in the agency feel I'm a role model, and I've got to make the part-time thing work because they want to have the chance.'

And Karen:

'What has given me more satisfaction than anything else was to use my power to promote a deputy from within the school. She was nowhere when I came. I like to think I recognised her potential. Under my male predecessor, she wouldn't even have applied. But I pushed her to do it, and because she trusted my authority – that means she believed I knew what I was talking about – she did it, got the job, and it makes me feel great.'

These powerful women are also very clear about how power should be used. Sheila says:

'I'm not interested in power for the sake of power, but for the good it can do. I am interested in that. I want to use it to make situations better, companies better, for the people in them. And to have the ability to do that through power. And to make my own choices, which no one can impose on me.

'I don't think I need people to know I've got power. At the end of the day it's nice when people think highly of you because of what you do, not what you say you do. You can't buy respect, or credibility, or trust – you earn them. And things you earn that way are more valuable and lasting. People trust me, and that gives me power.'

Sarah, too:

'I like having power as the boss. I'm not bossy. I like working with a team of people you can promote. I really want them to succeed. When I was promoted from merchandising manager, I took on someone who did the job better than I did. It didn't matter because I was her boss, and I was directing her, and I thought that you end up with a team of experts in various fields and better than me at all those functions, and all I have to be is general manager. I don't feel threatened, I feel I'm using my power properly. I'd be abusing it to employ less good people to protect my position.

'I like power. It means I can make decisions, not make people do my bidding. I don't think I exercise it in that way.'

Loneliness of Power

Women are no longer afraid of saying they have power. They no longer feel wary of saying they like it. All successful women have to believe in their own power. It is the public symbol of their success – much more so than money or title. Even today, though, a senior woman may well have to make a deliberate show of using her power before female and male colleagues believe in the reality of it.

With some women, there was a specific moment when they knew they had crossed the line of feminine demarcation between powerlessness and power. In Ellen's case, for instance, it was when a senior male colleague had to ask her to sign his expenses sheet:

'There was no one else he could go to at the time. He came into my office three times on flimsy errands before he asked me. He shoved the form in front of me and gave me a pen with the cap carefully stuck on the blunt end so I couldn't lose it. I didn't say anything about it, but I felt wonderful. Really equal.'

For Valerie, the moment came when she found she no longer had anyone to go to lunch with:

'Your first taste of power comes with your first senior management position, and as a woman it's very lonely when you suddenly realise you actually haven't got any-one to go to lunch with any more. Once you've got that bit of power, it just doesn't happen that you go with juniors. Until the senior guys get used to you they don't even think of suggesting you pop across to the pub for a drink.

'I think power comes with seeking responsibility, and it gets easier with practice. The common words used in relation to a woman when she's powerful are aggressive, bitchy. But look at her behaviour, and if a man did it, how would you judge it? Forceful. In my first years in manage-

ment, I used to go home heartbroken at some of the things
that went on. In the first line management job everyone
gets at you – other girls who work for you don't like it
because why should you be any different from them? The
guys above think, "She's just a woman".'

Power makes demands on women, too. Karen says:

'I feel I have to cope with power. It makes me feel very
awkward sometimes. I'm not the sort of person who wants
to exercise power over people. That doesn't mean to say
that when push comes to shove I won't dig my heels in and
say OK, we've talked about this, and this is how it's going
to be. That's very rare. I never sought out the power as
such.'

Women can find it awkward and embarrassing to pull rank.
Their management vision of teamwork scarcely allows them
to do so without seeming to fall short of their own standards.
Instead, they are evolving techniques for imposing their new
authority. Some, like Ellen, watch the way men jockey for
power at board meetings:

'They treat each other in quite a different way from the
way they behave to me. Sometimes it's extreme politeness,
sometimes extreme arrogance – but I've noticed that in
either case it depends on the way I behave. They're polite
to each other when I get shirty or adamant or thump the
table. Then I sail through getting what I want because they
think, "She must feel strongly about that, it's not worth
challenging her . . ." But where I'm not involved the men
start dancing up and down and it's a fight. It's irritating and
laughable at different times.'

When Power Means Having to Take Tough Action

However altruistic successful women's aims in exercising power, in practice it can be painful. Power implies responsibility, and powerful women can affect, for good or ill, the lives of those associated with them. They control other people's means of earning a living. At a time of recession, they must inevitably hand out redundancy. At least then there is the greatest good of the greatest number to consider, and an outside agency to blame. But most successful women have also had to fire staff for incompetence, incompatibility, or some other reason that boils down to personal failure. Sally agonised over it, and still feels guilty:

'Interpersonal relationships are very difficult for me, for a start. It was in my own business, and we were going down the chute. I had to make someone redundant. But I'd brought her in from a safe job. She'd moved flat to join me – changed her life. And recession hit us. It was very hard to do. I'd tackled things like theft in the office, and that's hard, too. There's a technique to these things. I'd learned it, but though knowing what to do is a help, how to do it and doing it take a lot more.

'Women at senior levels in business are very isolated at work, and there's no one there to talk to. I take it home and talk to my husband, but it's still something I find painful.'

On the other hand, one of the first difficult management decisions Karen made was to start dismissal proceedings against one of her teachers:

'It's a long-drawn-out process of warning letters and so on. I have no doubts that what I'm doing is right because this teacher is actually doing damage through incompetence. It's not a question of feeling sorry or trying to overlook mistakes because of the suffering involved. It's the children who are suffering, and I can't tolerate that. This teacher is a weak link in the team, and therefore all the other teachers are handicapped, both from having to try to put right the effects of mistakes later and from the undermining effect of what a thoroughly disaffected colleague says about me behind my back.

'I don't have any doubts about what I'm doing in this case. In other cases, I try to talk over a problem with someone who's not doing a good job – try to find out why, and if, with a bit of effort on both our parts, we couldn't get it right. There's one teacher I wouldn't let near older children, but she's good with the little ones. I would rather play to her strengths than fire her because she's got weaknesses.'

Board director Valerie, whose company is involved in redundancy counselling, believes that the ultimate test of how women practise power is how they deal with making staff redundant:

'I think women do it better. For men, so much of their identity is tied up with work that the man doing the firing is perceived – and may even perceive himself – as victor in some competition. He's won, the other has lost. Although a woman often sees redundancy very much as a personal rejection – they don't want *me* any more – women doing the firing can keep the competitive aspect out of it. Women give more thought to what they are going to say, and their sympathy is very genuine. Men just get gruff and it all gets depersonalised. Women have found a way of dealing with power without losing personal touch with the people they have power over – and they don't feel guilty about it any more. Inexperienced women who haven't learned that are a menace. They don't know the rules. Then they're the ones in tears, and it's a real mess.'

When it comes to exercising their power over people in practice, women admit that they treat men and women differently. Power involves setting standards for others, and the crunch often comes in handing out criticism. Valerie is very aware of this:

'I talk differently to men and women. I'm more circumspect about how I talk to women in business than I am with men. I'm much, much more direct with men. They interpret what you say differently. I don't think it's an aspect of rivalry; I think men are more direct anyway. Women tend to go more round the houses. If I want to tell one of my male colleagues I'm not happy with something he's done, then I'll say so directly. If I'm talking to one of the women who works for me, I'll go round it more. It comes to the same thing, but it takes longer. This difference arises out of wanting to avoid the emotional issues that will go with it more frequently with females than with males. A woman takes it personally: it's part of her make-up – but a man will too, particularly from a woman.'

Training director Ellen – the only woman director on the board of the company she works for – also recognises that she exerts her authority differently according to whether or not there are other women at a meeting:

'If it's all men, I approach them differently. I expect there will be competition, high determination, and the need to demonstrate quite forcibly that I'm in charge. With a group of women, I would expect much more co-operation, not combat, and no one would be wanting to win at the expense of everyone else.'

Karen is particularly careful with women not to damage their self-esteem, which – she takes it for granted – will be frail:

'I've got a woman member of staff who finds it hard to manage her class. She talks on top of the kids, and because she can't make her voice louder, it just gets higher and she screeches. I've told her again and again, and though I want to slap her face, I just come at it very gently, and she rushes away and weeps and nothing happens. It's easier to go for men. They're further away from you, there's a bigger distance between you. I feel women can't help it. Maybe with a woman you can see some of the feelings you've managed to overcome in yourself, and they are displaying them. I couldn't get cross with a woman who didn't want to do something on her own, for instance. There's an awful little-girl syndrome . . . maybe I'm hurtful because I put them down for being like that. It makes things worse as a boss because my job is to empower them, and give them confidence.'

Chief executive Sarah plans what she has to say carefully:

'It's not so much a difference between men and women, but people react very differently. I have three senior women directors. We get on quite well because we like each other. It helps that I recruited them and started their careers. We're quite good friends; it's not an autocratic relationship. One cannot take criticism. She's very good, but if she makes a bilge of something she blames me. She can't say she's made a mistake. With another, everything's her fault.

'On balance, men don't like being criticised. I'm straight-forward – "We didn't do a good job". I had to learn to be straightforward. When I have something to say, I still don't find it easy. I write it down on a piece of paper, making points, and put it in a drawer of my desk and leave the drawer open to make sure I say the things. I always do it first thing in the morning so it doesn't prey on my mind. I come in at 8.30, having written the list of points before I go to sleep.

'As part of trying to build a happy company, if someone has done badly I tell them. I don't want anyone hanging round afraid they're doing badly. I have one man who wasn't getting to grips with things. Then his son died, and his staff were giving him the runaround. He's fifty-two years old. We worked together on what he was doing wrong, and now he's become a director. He said no one had ever told him what he was doing wrong. He knew he wasn't coping, but no one ever told him and gave him the chance to put it right.

'I'm very conscious I can ruin somebody's life if I don't grasp the nettle of what they're doing wrong soon enough, because once it gets to the stage where everyone knows, they're really stuffed. I take the trouble to sort it out with them.

'There's one man – every time a woman goes in his office, she comes out crying. Even if she's being promoted. He had taken me literally about telling people what they're doing wrong. He'd tell them they were getting a salary increase, but they weren't any good. He didn't do it to men. Now he's not allowed to see anyone without the personnel director being there.'

The way successful women exercise power is affected by their experience on the receiving end. Sarah describes a point where she, as the victim of abuse of power, colluded with the abuser:

'I'd been the rising star in the company in the provinces, and I was brought to head office. It is the only time in my life when I've felt someone was prejudiced against me. I don't know if it was because I'm a woman, but one guy didn't like me. He just thought I was awful and not very bright. And I reverted right back to silly little Sarah. I was desperately unhappy. I could feel I was failing, and I couldn't do anything about it. I've met the guy since and he said, "I really made a mistake about you", but I said I wasn't so sure, because I behaved as he expected. He thought I was an idiot and I behaved like an idiot, though I was well aware I wasn't doing a good job. It was a very male company, and a lot of men who'd encouraged me were very worried. They kept asking if I was having boyfriend trouble, or was I going out with a married man?

'I thought it was my fault. The man was unfair, but I'd colluded. I can't say he treated me unfairly after the initial unfairness, and I did the rest to myself. I always felt I'd got where I was with a fair bit of luck, and I thought my luck had run out. The only thing I know I do better than others is I work harder. I assumed it was intellect that let me down. But it was a great lesson to me when I came to exercise power. I think men are much more likely to put a downer on people. Women are more encouragers. Men come and say so-and-so is useless, but I say shouldn't we do this or that – and in my experience, that has paid off. I know how it is to feel isolated like that because I had no female colleagues or friends I could talk to – and my failure meant someone else's success, so my immediate peers didn't mind if I sank without trace because it made things easier for them.'

Sarah believes that her experience as a victim of power abuse makes her more sensitive and effective in her exercise of power over others. In fact, women see themselves as abusing power chiefly by failing to exercise it. Sarah remembers one instance where she feels she was guilty of this:

'I went out with a guy when I worked with him. It was stupid, but we were both single. It finished peacefully. Then he worked for me, and I had to sack him. Definitely the sacking had something to do with the relationship, because he obviously hadn't been very good all the time, and I'd been doing his job for him. In the long term, I did him no favours by being too soft. If I'd revealed him earlier, he would have been younger and could have got another job. My misplaced niceness helping him do his job was actually me trying to help myself. I put off trying to sack him. It kept me awake at night. It wasn't just that I did his job, but his peers must have known. That's a double problem because they're thinking, "He doesn't get sacked because he's a friend of Sarah's". That taught me a lesson.'

Certainly female bosses who exercise power at work find that women have their own ways of deflecting evidence of other women's authority. Valerie says:

'Where I'm not good is where I encounter women who aren't competent at what they're doing, and they use the fact that they're female as an excuse. I can't help it, I can't stand it. I've no time for it at all. I'm not good if they cry. There was one woman in a board meeting, and she burst into tears while I was talking. I just walked round the table, picked up a tissue and gave it to her and carried on talking. All my male colleagues were sitting there wondering what to do. Some of them said later that I'd been harsh, but tears had nothing to do with the issue in hand. They were designed to deflect us from the issue and were frankly irrelevant. It was an excuse for not having done something. She went straight into the emotional aspect, but it took us nowhere. I've no time for anyone who can't take responsibility for what they have or haven't done.

'I have to take criticism too. I'll take out what's valid, discard the rest, and try not to be too sensitive. It gets easier as you go along. Bits rankle, though. But it's dangerous to see someone who criticises you as an enemy. At the end of the day, you don't have to like the people you work with. I prefer to, but don't have to. I learned that early, and it takes a lot of heat out of it. You don't have to be liked, either, though as a woman you spend your life trying to please people.

'I find it easier now to criticise others than I did ten years ago. I've had more practice, but I find it true that because I've now got a reputation for being very straightforward, and people expect me to be forthright, it's easier to give criticism. When I wasn't sure of the role I should play or how to conduct myself, I tended to be very nice, very easy-going, and people would look shocked when I had to say something wasn't on. My mentor told me to let people know where I stand. People are buying you as an honest individual. If they know you're saying what you are because you have the good of the business at heart, and really mean it, then they'll take it. That's good advice. Now nobody looks surprised when I say I'm not happy about something. I watch a lot of women and see they're angry but they won't say anything. They won't say what's not acceptable. If someone thinks her boss was cross and didn't say so, she's not comfortable with that because she couldn't defend herself. And she sees the boss as lacking courage, which introduces an area for manipulation. Women are the worst for recognising weakness in other women and using it to their advantage. With females, women recognise more the weaknesses of not managing a situation. With men, they recognise more weaknesses like – if they smile, does it have this effect? If I laugh at their jokes, what happens? Women learn how to manipulate the whole relationship. With women, it's really going for the weak spot – and a woman's weak spot is usually that she doesn't know what to do in terms of managing.'

Knowledge and Confidence

The successful exercise of power demands two vital prerequisites: knowledge and confidence. They are complementary, one growing from the other. Without both these essential elements, it is impossible to communicate authority. Andrea describes how her own initial insecurity made it impossible for her to manage staff effectively:

'For five years, I took everything on myself because I found delegating very difficult. Good management is altogether about mutual confidence and trust, and for me getting to the point to make help possible was a problem. If you do everything, what tends to happen is that you become unhelpable. No way can you allow help, because you can't present what's required in a way anyone else can make sense of. I've learned that through all sorts of difficulties with my first assistants. I was a very difficult employer to start with. I tried to tell them so much I swamped them. I had totally wrong expectations. The whole tool of language had to be rediscovered. What you know is one thing; what you have to convey is another. I was constantly writing things down, finding I'd been misunderstood and getting in a frightful state, and then reading what I'd written and finding it was me. I learned to write short notes. I used to write pages.

'I made mistakes with staff. Mostly I didn't know enough to know what I wanted. Setting up and running a successful business has given me an education. Every step I've taken has been a process of learning something new, and learning what you didn't know before gives you confidence. One vital thing I've learned is: it's impossible to learn anything until you need to know. Only the need to know will make you know it. I'm completely different now because I'm confident. When you're ignorant, you suspect everything and everybody and think everyone suspects you. They don't.'

Traditional male-dominated corporate structures have always cast women as the guardians of information – as secretaries and filing clerks, they organised and administered it. But their purpose was also to restrict the flow of power-giving information according to the status of the recipient. The more senior a manager, the more information he was allowed access to. But in practice, some senior women feel that they suffered because the women distributing information were unwilling to acknowledge their superior status. They may also be excluded by male colleagues: Valerie felt this particularly when she became a senior manager for an international hotel chain. She says:

'Much of the maleness of the business culture is about information. Men inform each other in pubs, in the gents', etc. What do women do? They tend to have to be more direct. If they want information they have to ask for it, and men aren't very good at saying no in that sense. But for a woman it's difficult to know what you want until you know what's to be known, so you can only find out by being around and listening.'

Sally claims that for her the most important source of authority was knowledge gained from the experience of being powerless:

'Authority comes from knowing. For a woman that's knowing what's important, and what your priorities are. It comes from experience. I've had lots of failures. My first marriage failed, and a relationship after that. Then my own business. I hate it. I took the blame on myself, but that's helpful because if you think there's nothing you could have done, you don't learn anything. You go on making the same mistakes. The worst thing is the expectation that it will be repeated. I think it's true of a lot of women that they're not prepared to take risks – they think they're failures, and take all the blame. It took a long time to convince myself that no one thought less of me because of failure, that I was still a valuable person. You make yourself out of the ordinary by being successful, and that gives you the confidence to make decisions.'

Sarah, too, includes what she calls passive knowledge as part of her power base:

'I'm very aware of people's characters, which is necessary for a good manager. I can see when they're worried, and how they get on. I know who gets on and who doesn't, who's laughed at behind their backs. I know when relationships start before they happen. Basically, I'm nosy. I like to know what's going on. I get my information through observation.'

Women with confidence in their own knowledge – and that includes knowing that they are able to do the job well – inspire the trust of colleagues. This is an important dimension for ambitious women, because the trust of others causes them to raise their game. Such mutual trust is important, because if the ambitious and successful can include such traditional interpretations of womanhood in the new gender-balanced business framework they are developing, they may manage to increase all women's potential access to power. If they can keep that common ground between themselves and other women, there is less likelihood that powerless women may be excluded from the process of change. It is already a considerable achievement that female-style interdependence and co-operation are now recognised as prerequisites of conventional management theory.

The effect is already obvious in the way the younger generation of businesswomen can assume power without any conflict between their personal and public persona. Janet sees an evolutionary victory in the difference between herself and young women now working for her in management roles:

'They need you to learn from. At the same time, they have no doubt that they have something you need. It makes assessments with females, if anything, more productive than with men. You tell them what they've done wrong, and then ask what you should be doing to help them. And they come straight out with it – you don't allow them enough rope, give them elbow room, they should have their own rights to organise their own work.'

Language

Women have an immediate problem with the language of power in business anyway: the life it reflects is based on male-only terms. Carol Gilligan's research supports the premiss that men and women may speak a different language that they assume is the same. They use similar words to encode quite disparate experience of self and social relationships.

I suggest that you can see this in the different way men and women use 'I' and 'you'. When women speak of 'I' in business terms, they mean 'we'; men mean 'me'. Women say 'you', meaning 'us'; men mean 'them'. Aspiring women can mistranslate these terms; this leads to a breakdown in communication and deprives them of a source of knowledge. Many women have tried to 'learn' to communicate on a man's terms. Valerie tried to communicate with male colleagues in their own language:

> 'It was the only way I could see of demonstrating I was on the team on my own merits, not because the managing director fancied my backside. All my jobs have been around male-dominated industries, so I got used to speaking their language. I emphasised what I meant for effect that way. It's the only way you can break in. Rightly or wrongly, I feel the onus is on the woman to break the circle.'

And Sarah says: 'Once I achieved a position of power, I noticed I started to swear more and sound coarse and use words stronger than I would naturally use.'

The French Prime Minister, Edith Cresson, recently talked about how social systems have a predominant language which perpetuates power cliques. This applies to business, too. In France, she says, it is the language of 'technostructure', and it is a kind of code:

> 'Naturally women will eventually be able to use it, but it is foreign to their personality. Women speak in a more ordinary way which is clearer and more readily understood.

Men, however – and often men of power – use a language which is difficult to understand but which is the coded language of the dominant class. Since women don't like this language, and it does not belong to them, they have difficulty in making themselves heard effectively.'

There are signs that a new terminology is emerging. It may rely on neuter jargon phrases like 'mission statements' and 'interactive' and 'empowerment'. The developing language of a gender-balanced business culture will tend to be the language of sexless technology. Ironically, it would seem as though as the business system becomes more gender-balanced and humane, the only language available to express this new humanity is borrowed from technology. Training director Ellen says:

'The confrontational terms of the language are changing, but another aspect is the language between men and women. Language between men is very different from language between women. Men swear at each other and don't talk about their families to other men, but they do to women. Men's attitude to women's language means that if women swear, they get upset. I'm always very provocative about that. I tell them it's just bullshit.'

Controlling Their Own Lives

At the same time, this new confidence gained in the workplace is changing women's expectations in their personal lives. Many successful women mentioned that power has given them control over their own lives. Lisa argues that because she gained power from her career rewards and status to control her whole life, rather than just the working part of it, she retains that power even while her career is on hold while she brings up her baby:

'I do like to be in control of my own destiny and other people's.

'There's an aspect of power in my wanting to bring up the child, even down to silly things. I want to teach her to swim. I want to be in control of how it's done. It's neither here nor there as long as she can swim, but it matters to me. I suppose I think I can do it best, but more than that, I can do it my own way.'

The ability to use power denotes maturity. In the process, women have revealed that the power men traditionally claimed was too often adolescent bullying rather than grown-up exercise of authority. Once women have gained the confidence to accept their own interpretation of power to enable and co-operate as part of their working and domestic lives, men's concept of it appears narrow and, ultimately, irrelevant in contrast.

Power can be constructive for women, as Lorraine says:

'I do think that being a successful working woman has a major impact on your confidence and how you present yourself. I can see it in myself, when I meet people I was at school with. I wasn't particularly cleverer than they were, or more talented, but now, because I'm involved in the world of work, I've learned to be succinct when I speak. I've learned how to organise myself, how to speak out and expect people to listen to me. You know what you are capable of, and that gives you a sense of power. Now it's become part of me as a woman.'

4

COMPETITION:
BLOOD ON THE GLASS CEILING

I N a profit-based business culture, the road to success is paved with competition. The system is overtly confrontational and divisive, with every step upward and onward seemingly made over the bodies of defeated career-dead. Most successful women in business see this approach – as though every issue is a jousting match for the corporate king's favour – as both destructive and wasteful.

On the other hand, now that the male system is being called into question in many of the country's top companies, women are coming up against some deep-seated inhibitions about their own competitiveness.

Competition with Goliath

In competition with men and the masculine-dominated hierarchies, women are the underdogs, and it is safe – either they are Davids defeating Goliath, or, if Goliath wins, the odds were so stacked against them at the start that they emerge as heroines anyway. Sarah says:

'At the start of my career, I felt very competitive with men. I felt I did the work as well as they did. I still feel more competitive with men than with women. I felt proud at beating men, and that was an incentive to keep pushing forward.'

All successful women have learned to relish competing against men – and beating them. As Janet says:

'I've always got along well with the women who work for me, but I handle them by saying, "Watch me and do as I do". I've never thrown my weight around except with men, because men challenged me much more. I've never felt competition with people below me, but I've had desperately hard times competing with men above me.'

But the nature of competition is changing. Michael – who, as training director of a computer combine, has set up a Think Tank to study management change – explains:

'Management theory is moving away from the idea of hope and reward to encourage being open and direct rather than competing. A lot of people are questioning whether there's any need to be so overtly competitive – or, indeed, if they can continue to support a high degree of competitiveness within an organisation. Certainly competition within the organisation used to be the way things were done, but we can't do it now. We simply can't afford to. We are no longer in such a rapidly growing market, so we can't afford to have a highly competitive internal climate. Now we must concentrate on competing with our industry rivals, not within the organisation.'

Marginalisation no Longer

There was a time when men seemed to counter women's push towards equality in management by isolating areas where women tended to be most successful in competition for jobs. These areas were then downgraded as 'women's specialities', and ambitious men did not enter them if they could help it. In the process, these areas of women's interest lost professional standing. In Russia, this has happened with the medical profession, where doctoring is now almost exclusively 'women's work', and consequently seen as a low-grade career.

In the UK, personnel, marketing, public relations and training as fields of management expertise used to be marginalised in the same way, but no longer. The current trend in business as a whole makes particular demands on these areas, which are the very ones that exemplify the new emphasis on communication and human resources in corporate thinking. The women involved have transcended the professional standards originally laid down by men. They have learned to compete on their own terms for their areas of interest. The recession has helped, perhaps, because it has meant that no business function can be downgraded as a soft option – corporate survival has come to depend on high standards of professionalism in all these areas. Now good management seeks to capitalise on people's strengths, rather than use their weaknesses to rule by fear.

Ellen is a training director in a male-dominated system where top management is beginning to realise they cannot survive without a change of attitude towards fields they had previously not seen as important. Training is one:

'Part of male competitiveness is that they keep knowledge to themselves if they can – on the principle you don't help the opposition even if they're on the same team. In some ways,

113

training has a maternal quality – the reason why there are so many women in a training role is because they want to pass it on. The male attitude to me involves their attitude to training and to women – that they can both be done without. It adds to the non-positive pressure that I'm on the line, and so's my profession. That links with needing to fight for every penny and every minute to be given to training. If left to themselves, some of these men would cut back training and women, but now there's a growing belief from the top of this organisation that training is crucial to the future and, other things being equal, we should go for the woman.'

Women versus Men's Ways

Women's problem is that when they must compete at work, it is on men's confrontational terms. Men, for instance, almost always talk in terms of competing *against*, while women compete *with*. As the business climate shifts away from male-dominated systems, we can expect the concept of competitiveness in its macho guise to change with it. But women in sufficient numbers to effect change are still a new phenomenon in top management, and they are only just beginning to evolve a way of competing with men and other women on their own terms.

Sheila, brought up by a strong mother, had no youthful competition from her brother. He never intended to leave their close-knit mining community, and he never saw education as the way out, as she did. She believes that competitiveness against men – or at least, the male system – is implicit in any woman's drive for success:

 'Do women have to get equality at the expense of men? I wish I could say I disagreed, but I think it's true. The danger now is the backlash. While men are still in a majority in senior positions, that backlash can be made to work. I think that if there's enough for all in the general economy, we can get degrees of flexibility which will take the heat out of men's self-preserving competitiveness, but when times are hard they can band together to change the bases of competition, and women will suffer.'

In her book on competition between women, *The Secret Between Us*, published in 1991, American academic Laura Tracy describes an experiment looking into the difference between the ways boys and girls played games. She found that boys' games lasted much longer than girls'. Though boys quarrelled all the time, they sorted out their differences and went on with the game. If there was a dispute between girls, they all immediately stopped playing.

Management consultant Lorraine thinks that seeds of competitive inadequacy are sown early in girls:

'From childhood, boys are set against boys in a way girls aren't. In business, men carry that on, but women have to learn to be confrontational. It's easier to confront men now, because as a gender we are angry with them, but it holds women back. On management courses, women don't speak as much as men. There's no doubt about that. There's no question that in classes I encourage them. I think: God, I'm one of the few women who's going to teach them, why shouldn't they get a better time with me? But I get very bad feedback from some of the men. Some of the women tell me that they get the feeling the guys groan if they start speaking. I've also heard that when I walk in for the first time, there's a slight feeling it's a second-class part of the course. Women find it difficult to work in some of the groups because they don't get their voice heard.'

Joan started her own property management business because she saw that as a way of doing things her way, without having to overthrow an existing male-biased system, and she did not want to dilute her domestic self to conform to corporate convention.

Ellen, on the other hand, was attracted to management because she wanted to confront a male world:

'You know what you're getting into, though men's attitudes are changing, and with more women at higher levels, they have had to tone down some of their outrageous chauvinism. I had an innate attraction to the combative system, and an innate belief I could do the job well. I suppose I had the bossyboots approach, wanting to get things sorted out, getting pleasure out of getting things moving. That was inherent.

'But I can't deny my approach to management is different. Men's is to climb the ladder, and a lot see things in terms of helping their own career. I often feel that if I don't get it right, it will have a negative impact on my credibility and personal position. I feel my personal credibility is always on the line, so I've got to get it right.'

Here again, though, there are signs that young achievers have a different approach to competition with men than their predecessors. Sheila (in her late thirties) says:

'The previous generation seemed to feel that they couldn't give themselves permission to take equality at work as a right, even though they wanted it. Something built-in made them feel they had to apologise for wanting it, or be grateful to men for letting them try to get it.

'As financial director on the main board of a large company, I see myself as a businessperson first and a woman in that situation second. I probably do bring a different approach on the board. I hope I do. I'd hate to deny my femaleness, but I am what I am and I act in a particular way. I think people have different degrees of male and female within them. I love being a woman, but I can be very hard if I have to. I'm probably harder than most women if I have to be for the good of the business, or if it's necessary for the good of people as a whole.'

Certainly women find that competing with women is quite different from their competitions with men. Until very recently men in business would not acknowledge that their work relationship with women involved competition. Instead, they attacked. So women often feel that when men compete against them, they are under attack. They go on the defensive because they recognise an enemy. Joan says:

'I find women much easier to work with, but that's because the way I work, stringing out a series of ideas and then jumping backwards, drives men mad. The only time I've had bother with competitiveness was once when a man tried to take over my position. The way he did that was to work behind my back to devise a structure by which he'd be number one and I'd be number two.'

When she organised her breakfast discussions for business-women at the Treasury, Gillian Shephard found that all her guests mentioned how productive and far-ranging the meeting had been because it was women-only:

'Some had not been to an all-woman meeting before. They were impressed at how quickly we got down to business, with no posturing, no showing off. They felt men show off. Ours wasn't a competitive meeting, and they felt that was because there weren't any men. They thought we got through a lot more work in a much more direct way. They felt they worked better without men to waste time.'

What these women are really saying is not that men show off when there are women at a business meeting. They are saying that they behave differently, too. Many very successful women would admit that their competitive reactions still reflect domestic conditioning. When men, particularly senior men, are part of a business meeting, women tend to fall back on traditional expectations that girls show off in front of men they want to impress, from Daddy to boyfriends. That, for them, is the proven route to future security. And inevitably, their reaction to the men sets the regressive tone of the competitiveness between the women.

The challenge for women is to find a way of transposing the competitiveness they learned at home – the kind which protects other women from a sense of failure – into a confrontational workplace where competition is designed to select winners and discard losers. The self-confidence involved in taking such a risk is easier to describe than to win. Personnel director Julie tells a typical story:

> 'An employer advertised for a senior manager, who had to have high educational qualifications, experience, skills as a communicator and leader. The salary offered was £50,000 a year. He had several hundred applicants, nearly all men.
>
> 'As an experiment, he advertised exactly the same job, same qualifications necessary – exactly the same wording. But the salary offered was £10,000 a year. He had several hundred applicants, all women.
>
> 'I think the issue is that in any competitive situation – which business is – a good woman will have a lower opinion of herself than a good man. Women not only undervalue themselves, but they tend to play more on their

weaknesses. Assertiveness training can help – and younger women have a lack of fear, and don't see a problem where older women do.'

Women versus Women

When it comes to work, women have no blueprint for competition. They cannot simply stop playing if there's a problem. Successful women don't, as part of their business life, play games of one-upmanship like squash and golf and poker. Instead, they go to lunch with each other, shop with each other, socialise together – few outlets for overt competitiveness. For men, their games are part of proof of supremacy, where the loser is inevitably defeated and counted out. Two men of equal status will fight to the point of heart failure to win a game of squash! Their subsequent status in the office will be influenced by the result of the game.

In contrast, two women playing tennis will both try to win, but often the winner will instantly give her defeated opponent an excuse for losing. Women are usually embarrassed to see another woman lose. They gain nothing from humiliating each other. Men apparently do.

This goes back to the traditional conventions of women as supportive, enabling, nurturing. Women have nowhere to go for their models for competitiveness except family life, where competition is limited by domestic imperatives like keeping the peace and looking after others. Girls may compete with their sisters for their parents' attention, but it's in the context of the sure and safe knowledge that no one's security will be threatened as a result. They compete with their friends for boyfriends, perhaps, but until they are successful, this is a competition where they tend to be supported by at least one other girl who is unequivocally on their side. Their competitiveness becomes a group issue. They compete with their mothers for their own identity, but on the assumption that their mothers will love them anyway.

This old domestic level of competitiveness between women still haunts the workplace. Here is the source of the threat older women feel from the younger high-fliers on their corporate heels. For many women, to compete with another woman in a work context involves a degree of betrayal. It is only very recently that society has allowed women to 'qualify' as women when they deliberately flout the conventions of traditional womanhood to achieve success.

Take the Queen Bee syndrome, for example – the lone women who clawed their way to the top of the male heap in corporate structures throughout the Western world, and shut the door firmly on any aspiring females climbing the ladder behind them. The Queen Bee is probably everything other women have ever said or thought about her, but almost certainly she has received nothing to feel grateful for from other women on her way up.

In their eyes, what she did was repudiate her womanhood. There was no place for the current conventions of femininity in the business culture, so the virtues and values of the universal female were expected to wither and die in her from lack of use. When she became the token woman in the masculine system, her male colleagues tacitly repudiated her femininity. Other women disallowed it. They saw her as a better man than the men. Though Janet, founder of her own research company, would deny that she ever blocked another woman's path, she knows she was called a Queen Bee by junior colleagues, and how isolated she felt:

'I was disliked. I was marked down by male and female colleagues as uncaring and unfeeling because I was completely committed to my career. I didn't like that, but I buried it away. What I still wanted was a really quality research company – something of my own – and to prove it was possible to do it by running it in a more businesslike and professional way. I was driven. It was overwhelming, more important than children or my first marriage. Other women? It was terrible. They thought I was weird for working like I did. I minded very much that they cut me out for years – until that crop decided *they* should have jobs. At work it wasn't quite so bad because I surrounded myself with like-minded people. Yes, they did tend to be men – of course they did, because at that time it was men who had the qualifications to do the job. But even then, and certainly now, I would practise positive discrimination in favour of women who could do the job. And no, I didn't enjoy my lone status. It's terrible not to have female friends you can talk to.'

As a middle manager, Suzanne, now a company director, was surprised at her own reaction when she found that a female colleague at work had put in for a promotion she had applied for:

'I couldn't believe it. I felt awful, as though I'd found she was having an affair with my husband. I couldn't think what I'd ever done to her that she was my enemy. We'd never been close, but we'd worked together for some months. Of course I knew this was irrational. In a way I knew I had done exactly the same to her. I even thought of withdrawing to preserve our friendship, but I thought I'd be letting her get away with something. In the end she took me out for a drink and told me she wanted the job. She said she knew I wanted it, too, and that gave us something more in common. And why should it make any difference

121

between us? Neither of us could think of any reason. It was the job we wanted, not to damage each other. She got it, and I feel closer to her now because we shared something quite intimate by competing.'

In the workplace, the growing dichotomy between the established and evolving framework for competitiveness has forced women to find ways to give themselves permission to compete with each other. All the time, more women are discovering that any domestic salve we smear over our growing competitiveness in the workplace is no longer adequate. The problem is that we have very, very few workplace role models for competitive behaviour between women and on women's terms.

The consensus view of a woman who makes no secret of her competitiveness is that she is a bitch. In fact, it is actually the group who condemn her who are demonstrating their own competitive behaviour. Nasty things are always said behind the back of the woman who is in some way pushing herself forward – that is, competing with other women. No one has a bad word for the woman who merges with the crowd. The group is competing negatively with the one who wants to set herself apart – competing for the security that comes from uncompetitive equality, however far down the heap.

On the whole, women do seem to seek to avoid confrontation when the competitive situation involves another woman. Sheila says:

'I will say, hand on heart – and believe it – that in business I'm not competitive. I know I am outside work, where my competitive nature comes out in very specific areas. For instance, I went go-karting with my brother, and some friends of his. I'd have died rather than lose. I'd no idea I'd feel like that. I don't in business. Yes, I probably would have disguised it if there'd been women there. I'd have been gentler about it. With most of the women I meet I have to be more female. I can go out and do it with men, and if I lose I walk away. If a man loses, he has problems with that loss. I don't have that desperation when I've given it my all, and don't win – well, OK, fine. With men, the balance of their professional relationship is fixed by competitive failure. In business, though, competitiveness isn't conscious.'

Karen can't come to terms with competing with women: 'I respect rather than compete with women. Competition would involve confrontation, and I'm too afraid of damaging very fragile female self-esteem.'

The price women have to pay for successfully competing against men is that they must now come to terms with competing with each other. As children, they found a framework for competitive games. They stopped the game when things got difficult between the players, because they were afraid of chaos. But the power they take from success in business enables them to control their lives. They need no longer fear chaos. Once they are confident of their ability to take control, they have a framework for competition.

Karen thinks women undervalue themselves in competitive situations:

'It seems to me as though the only way they can give themselves permission to compete against each other is to show they expect to fail. At times I think they want to fail to let themselves off a hook. They can show they made the effort to meet new demands of womanhood, but it's easier to let somebody else take the responsibility of winning. If you win, you have to carry the can for decisions; if you

123

don't, someone else makes the decision, and you can complain.

'Women are very unwilling to push themselves forward. Competition is confrontation, and their self-esteem isn't good enough to allow them to do it. They seem to play themselves down as though to defray attack. When I was interviewing for the job as my deputy, there were four shortlisted candidates. Two women were miles ahead of the two men. But at interview, both men managed to say they'd got wives and two kids and had reached a point in their career where they thought they were ready for deputy headship. The women had both had to be pushed to apply. What inhibits them is not seeing themselves in that role, because they don't have the role models. I had to convince my deputy that she could do the job once she'd got it.

'When women do push themselves forward, they have a friend to support them. It's the way I work at school. I get on very well with my deputy, and we work as a team. We don't do things in isolation. I won't take a decision unless I've discussed it with her. What women need to do is find a way of competing where they don't feel that they are dividing themselves from other women.'

Women often have a problem with competition because they see other women's success as a comparable put-down for themselves – 'She was chosen, therefore I was rejected'. This can happen when a senior woman resents successful younger women who, they think, have had an easier ride than they did. Valerie says:

'The only person who set out to block me was a woman. She was much older – forty to my twenty-one. She dug a hole for me at every opportunity. At first I was very naive and didn't see it. It was all very friendly – "Come on,

Valerie, I'll help you with this or that" – and then I'd find myself landing in a situation and know I'd been set up. It made me very wary for a long time of other women in management. She always did it on the basis that she was my best friend there and I could trust her.

'There's less of that kind of thing now that women will compete with each other openly. Now women moving up the ranks are quite comfortable with the competition side – you'd find they score quite high on competition and achieving. Women competing with women tend to pussy-foot a bit in case it's seen as bitchiness, not being sort of all pals together.'

Essentially, while women see each other's competitive success as personal rejection, they are going to see all competition as hostile. Fortunately, many successful women have gained the maturity to ignore it. Valerie has a problem with a junior member of her staff who cannot bring herself to acknowledge that Valerie is her boss:

'She won't refer to me as her boss. I find it very funny. In all her reviews and assessments, she treats me as her boss, but she can't say the words. If she has to identify herself over the phone, she says she's a colleague of mine.'

Lorraine, too, has grown more confident since the competitive hostility of her youth:

'I managed about thirty consultants in my first management job. The only two who gave me any trouble were women. One was older than me, and when she joined I told her she would be reporting to me – did she understand that's the situation and accept it? Within six months she was being very difficult and undermining me. The other woman was in her twenties, the same age as me, and there was jealousy on both sides. She had an affair with my mentor.

'If I look at times in my twenties, I was very competitive, just as much with women as men. There was just one woman there and we competed with each other, and the men took enormous pride watching the two of us bitching. Now I'm more secure, and find women very supportive of each other. I think I was pretty difficult to live with at work in my twenties. Now it really pleases me to see women doing well at meetings.'

What we're also talking about here is jealousy. Until women are well established in the higher echelons of corporate management, jealousy is bound to play a significant part in the way they compete with each other. Unlike envy, which is the desire for something someone else has, jealousy stems from the fear of losing what we think we possess. Jealousy arises from insecurity.

In the workplace, even successful women are not yet secure enough in their management role to risk losing what they have gained by competition. They are possessive about what they have, and interpret competition from another woman as a hostile move. An obvious way to defray such an attack is to deny that they have won anything worth possessing.

Women try to avoid posing a threat to others by putting themselves down. They will deny their ambitions to defray jealousy. Because they know how painful it is both to be jealous and to have someone jealous of them, women are aware that competition between them is not the same as a direct challenge to male authority. Sally says:

'I compete differently with women than with men. I use different weapons. With men you use your very opposite-ness in being a woman, your femininity, whereas against a woman you're using the same weapons, so you're slightly sneakier, I suppose. It's tougher to redress the balance and become different. Women don't like competing against each other – it makes us very tense. Perhaps we don't know how to. In a limited way, women must train to compete. I worked in a firm run by women with lowly men. There was competition, but it was fairly subtle and manipulative. I can't think there was ever any open conflict – that is, until a male manager was introduced at a higher level to the team. He would come out with things we would have skirted round. We got used to it, but it didn't go down very well.'

There are grounds for hope that ambitious women in competitive situations are gradually becoming self-confident enough to refuse to see each other as enemies. Ironically, once the competitiveness goes out of enmity, they are free to dislike each other heartily without the guilt feelings associated with competition – there was always the suspicion that dislike came from sour grapes after losing, and was therefore something to be ashamed of. Or they can continue to like each other, because competition no longer involves the end of a personal relationship with the women they compete with. Sheila says:

'We don't take competition between us now as personally as a man protecting his progression. If you lose a fight, you lose. If you win more than you lose, you're ahead, but if you lose, lose well. I work on the principle that I'm part of a team. I don't have this fear of losing in that I don't see it as losing if the best decision is made for the purpose of moving the business forward. Men actually fear not winning as a personal failure.'

Old Conventions versus New Needs

Many successful women internalise the conflict between the old and the new conventions of what women want or need. Anne, for instance, having given up full-time work and turned to freelance part-time consultancy since her baby was born, finds that her feelings about work and the child compete – not just for her time and attention, either, but on a deep emotional level she is quite frightened to explore:

'The baby is sixteen months now, and up to now I feel she is the most important thing. What I do with my life has got to reflect her needs first – her emotional and social needs. I think the main thing is her emotional needs, and that it's important she should spend more time with me than with someone else. All I can do is provide offers of choice. This is where I feel at war with myself. Since the baby, the creativity I put into work has changed. To fulfil the role I see as being a good mother means that I have a full part to play in that work world, but my relationship with the baby competes with that.'

Anne finds it hard to articulate how her warring expectations about a woman's role affect the way she feels towards other women she is in contact with. She finds that both full-time mothers and full-time career women dismiss her internal conflict as lack of commitment to one or other definition of womanhood.

Businesswomen versus Those Not in the Game

As far as many women outside the workplace are concerned, there is an unsurmountable division between themselves and the ambitious female competitor. Women who do not work, or do not give high personal priority to their careers, can still undermine the successful businesswoman. Valerie – who, before running an executive recruitment agency, was the first woman on the main board of an international hotel and catering chain – describes her experience with colleagues' wives:

> 'When I became a line manager, the guys would all disappear to the pub, and they didn't ask me. When I became a director and they went to lunch without me, I just went with them without being asked. Apart from the ones who say initially, "You won't ever mention to my wife that you come to lunch with us", it got accepted.
>
> 'These men are usually right about the women they think they're married to. An awful lot of colleagues' wives have rung me up and said, "Just because you're going on a business trip with my husband, you needn't think you can steal him away from me." I've been tempted to tell them I wouldn't sleep with their husbands if they were the last men on earth. It's the assumption that by working on an equal basis with what they see as their property, you're making a bid for it. Actually, it's not just their property, is it? It's their life-support machine. Even so, I tend not to be sympathetic. It's a very personal attack because if they say that to you, they're judging you without getting to know you – in other words, they're saying you must be in your position not because you deserve to be, but because you're prepared to sleep your way up.'

Lorraine, on her way to becoming a senior management consultant, found that even men committed to encouraging and promoting women to senior positions pandered to their wives' and other women's potential hostility to a female high-flier:

'I had two senior mentors in the company. In both cases it was misinterpreted and the guys were very embarrassed. It was silly, because there was nothing to be embarrassed about.'

Valerie, though resentful of the wives' personal reaction, empathises with their rationale:

'Women like that see you as competition. You spend effectively more time with their husband than they do, and you probably see the best side of him, too. They are jealous.'

In the domestic arena, women possess very little that is their own, so it is not surprising that they will try to hang on to what they believe they do possess – their traditional role. Self-seeking and ambitious women who reject that role, or want to change it radically, are inevitably a threat to them. So successful women are often aware of resentment from less ambitious female friends, because in pushing themselves for promotion they are rejecting the sanitised competition of the domestic arena. Andrea felt this:

'There was a period when many of my women friends tried to put me off being in business. They wanted me back in the fold, and the idea that I could be successful like that was counter to everything they knew about me. I think what happens is that when people are successful, they're more confident, swifter in the way they deal with their lives, and make people who knew them in another mode feel insecure.'

Competing with the Team

In the workplace, though, many successful and ambitious women have evolved a framework for their competitive drive which does not alienate them from women colleagues. They have learned to compete *for* rather than *against*. They prefer to compete for each other, in a way – for the team, or recognition; for status for women in general, or their company's advantage over a rival. Sheila says:

> 'There aren't any other senior managers in the company who are women. Our women are mainly secretaries, and some junior managers. They don't envy my position. They say "good on yer!"'

And when I went to the Treasury to talk to Gillian Shephard, the middle-aged woman who guided me back from her office to the street said: 'What do you think of our Minister, then? Isn't she great? She's so nice and so good at her job, and it just makes you feel better to have her there.' Now I've visited Chancellors and male Ministers at the Treasury several times over the years, and never has either a man or woman guide asked afterwards what I thought of them. It does seem that at least women do not automatically see another woman's competitive success as some sort of personal belittlement of themselves.

The growth of women's networks supports this impression. Their success is an illustration of how women are colonising competitiveness between them. Men may react by trying to ghettoise women, as Ellen finds when she is called upon to take on the role of apologist for women's work problems in the company. That way, they can marginalise the competitive challenge women represent to them. Instead, competition between women has become part of the process of settling down as a team. Women compete to identify their territory within the group, but once that is done, they work together as a team. A newcomer to that team may well feel that the others are competing against her, but this is how individuals within a group define themselves, and how the team readjusts.

As women learn to compete without tearing themselves and each other apart, the nature of competition in its masculine sense changes, but competition is still a vital factor in business – even when the idea of competition is contrary to the *raison d'être* of the business – in a trade union, for example? Carol is a senior administrator in a union within the public service sector:

> 'In the office we are all so bound up with the common cause that we don't compete. I honestly don't think we do. For one thing, if a vacancy came up and I wanted it, even if someone else got it I would trust my boss had made a decision between us in the interests of the greatest good for the greatest number. Either he thinks she is better for the job, or he values the contribution I make where I am, and thinks I am more useful here. None of us would be working here anyway if we weren't prepared to make personal sacrifices so that the union can continue to help people. We would get paid far more, for instance, in the private sector.
>
> 'The only sense in which I think we may compete is with other unions for members. The more members we have, the more effective we can be in helping and fighting for them, so it's important to our success. I think that may be a reason why we don't compete with each other internally – we're competing so damned hard to keep our market share, if you like.'

Competition, then, can conform to the moral purpose embodied in women's management style. Sarah says:

> 'I don't mind if I hire men or women, as long as they're the best person for the job. I want people who are technically

competent, of course, but beyond that what's important is that they fit in with the team. In practice, that means I favour women, but it's not because I fear for my job. I really want them to succeed.'

When You Lose

In any competitive arena, there are bound to be losers. Business is highly competitive. Joan had a twenty-seven-year-old business rival who had already established her company when Joan set up in competition:

'She'd built it up from scratch. She had eight staff, a turnover of £17,000 a month. She had no doubts about herself at all. She was terrific at cold selling, and pushed after jobs. She was very, very generous to me when I started. She talked me through and guided me. I had nothing to offer her in return. Then, because of the recession, her business collapsed. She went through shock. Then I could repay her by listening to her and reboosting her. Part of her reaction was to think she could have put in more hours, worked harder, etc. She did see she had a personal responsibility for failure, but though she was semi-devastated, I was amazed at how cool she was. She sacked her eight staff and moved on, where I agonise. She doesn't have to ring any more.'

Women no longer enter competition with an alibi for failure culled from traditional concepts of womanhood. They have to bear personally the responsibility for losing. It seems that this often gives them an added determination to glean some-thing positive from failure. Sally, managing director of a training company, claims that she built her self-esteem out of the painful failure of her first marriage and the downfall of her own company, which has become part of the firm she now works for:

> 'Training is a competitive area of business, and I thought when the business failed there'd be a few women rivals who'd not be sorry. But it wasn't like that at all. Women I'd never met rang to commiserate. They told me they'd been through it, and I mustn't give up. They gave me the courage to start again. If that's competitive behaviour between women, it's bloody terrific.'

5

THE COLOUR
OF HER MONEY

THE business culture, as it becomes more female-
orientated, allows successful women to prove that they
have thrown off dependent womanhood and become fully
adult. That means independent, and the first test of independence is economic.

Money: Emotional Binds

The whole gist of the traditional concept of being female
demanded that a woman earned her living through caring for
and nurturing male breadwinners. Good little girls were
rewarded with pocket money from Daddy, or a sixpence from
Uncle; and the good little girl was the one who was sweet and
submissive and beguiling. She was probably expected to thank
him with a kiss. Later, an unexpurgated version of exactly the
same performance would wheedle financial life-support out
of a husband.

Some successful and high-powered working women have still not broken out of this emotional bind over money. One very high-powered and successful lawyer admits that in spite of a six-figure salary, she is always overdrawn at the bank. She fears that if she got to grips with her money, and showed that she could control it, she might become the kind of person her father would describe as unfeminine and off-putting to men:

'I go out on these shopping binges, where I buy all sorts of stuff I'm never going to need and don't want. I insist it's all packed and packaged very elaborately, and then I bring it home and open it in the sitting-room in front of a picture of my father. Can you believe it? I just sit there with all this useless and expensive stuff just to prove I can afford it without anyone's help. And then I give most of it away to people I don't even like because that takes the curse off it. Then I have to go to the bank manager to beg him to keep my overdraft going – which is obviously symbolic in some awful Freudian way. Perhaps I should try a woman bank manager.'

The average hourly wage for women is still only 73 per cent of men's. In fact, even though dual incomes, women promoted to high-earning jobs and rich women as role models are now commonplace, even successful businesswomen often still have a problem in talking about money, or asking for more – not just from men, either. It can be very difficult for one woman to ask another for more money, as Anne, a senior manager of thirty-nine, found:

'It was easier with a man. It was as though you tried to wheedle it out of him, and if he refused, you could blame him. But when I asked my woman boss for more money, because I'd taken on someone else's work, there was nothing to fall back on. For a start, you feel very pushy asking more for yourself, when so many women are underpaid – the old principle of eating school food because of the starving babies in Africa. And secondly, if she turns you down, you blame yourself because she would only do it if she thought you didn't deserve it. You can tell yourself she's just a bitch, or jealous of someone younger, but you know it comes down to being judged and found wanting as a woman by another woman.'

Money and Status

Yet financial recognition is central to women's status in business. Money measures how seriously they are taken on a professional level. A recent case before an industrial tribunal revolved around a £160,000-a-year pay package which a thirty-one-year-old City broker expected when she returned to work after having her baby. It got huge newspaper coverage, all in a tone of surprise that women could be considered worth such money, which in public perception is a measure of high professional respect.

Younger women themselves are less inhibited than their older female colleagues in putting a value on themselves and expecting it to be accepted. Lisa, the advertising agency director, says:

'It's very important to me to work in a meritocracy. Promotionally, there's no prejudice against women that I can see. I don't see myself playing corporate games in a traditional hierarchy. They turn me off with their grades. If I'm useless, I'll be fired. If I'm good, I'll get paid a lot. I like that. I only ever got angry in business once when I thought something was unfair. I joined the board in January when there had been a vacancy the July before, but I was told I hadn't been there long enough. I was furious. If they'd said I wasn't good enough, OK, but not been there long enough was ridiculous. People should do the jobs they can do. It's nothing to do with how long you've been there, or whether you're a man or a woman or black or white.'

Lisa admits that she enjoys the money she earns. She does not see that she should feel guilty because she earns more than she needs, and much more than most women. Money, flash cars, a high standard of living, being able to buy what you want because you want it – most successful younger women appreciate these rewards. They can set aside any ambivalence about 'deserving' them by telling themselves that they would not receive them if an authority figure did not believe them worthy. Only where there is a high moral or political purpose to work – in charities, for example, or unions, or enterprises like co-operatives – are material benefits not seen as particularly important. But Dounne says:

'All women, whatever our colour, have undervalued ourselves. By making money and being successful, we are providing a real role model to show other women it can be done.'

Valerie also sees the rewards of success as recognition signals which command the respect and acceptance necessary to build confidence. Without the display of these rewards, women are easily marginalised and ignored.

Lorraine recognises that the £1,500 a day she earns as a management consultant is a lot of money, but has no doubt that it reflects what she deserves. Sarah and Sheila control company budgets of £190 million and £150 million respectively. Janet is responsible for the livelihoods of hundreds, Sarah of thousands. But women can still be ambivalent about their relationship with money. It is the ultimate proof that they stand alone. Sarah, promoted chief executive from managing director, had initial doubts about taking the top job:

'All the other career steps I'd made, I'd known enough technically about what the job entailed. But I felt very daunted because I felt totally ignorant about money and the City, and I didn't think I could cope with it. I accepted in the end because the chairman pushed me, insisting I should do it because I did have these doubts, and it gave me an opportunity to learn something new.'

Valerie says she realises the fundamental part money plays in the relationship between men and women at work when junior male colleagues have difficulty dealing with her when money is involved:

'They come and ask me if this or that senior man will be back soon, but they won't ask me. I ask if they want expenses signing, and they say no. Why? They say they don't think I should. And I ask why – do they think I shouldn't have the job I do?

'My reaction is to take it as an insult, because it all goes back to women taking money from Daddy. Being in a position to dispense money to junior men is an important sign of my independence and success. I suppose they have problems because no real man ever took money from Mummy.'

What Money Says

In their private lives, earning a lot of money by their own efforts enables successful women to control their environment. They can choose where they want to live, take exotic holidays, expand their personal horizons – by learning to fly or playing polo or eating caviar, if they want to. They can avoid the hassles which beset ordinary women – queueing and public transport and being afraid to open household bills. But most of the women I talked to are ambivalent about this, too. They see their money dividing them from their common ground with ordinary women. Lisa, for example, is defensive:

'The money I earn buys lifestyle. This affects my aspirations for my child. You want to give them the opportunities you had. I want her to have the opportunity to do anything she wants. Politically I still have problems with private schools, but because we're in London I find it hard to imagine how I can not send her to public school. You can't sacrifice your child to a principle of yours.

'I don't have problems with making a lot of money *per se*. I think everyone should be entitled to good health and education, and after that it's up to them. It's wrong that money can buy you these things.

'Even so, I couldn't do something and just break even. I'd find that very frustrating. I've got to make enough money to make it worthwhile, which means enough to make me feel I'm in charge, master of my own destiny.'

Money: Ambivalence

Even so, some women still need to be given permission to spend their own money. Pam, head of her own public-relations company in Wales, employs her husband as her assistant. Since they married, ten years ago, she has kept their joint account with the bank. He has his own account, but any personal cheque she uses, he has to sign too:

'It sounds very silly, and a lot of people tell me I should stop it. I've got one friend who won't come shopping with me any more because I won't buy anything straight out. But I feel that when he has to sign, it involves him in the way the money's used. If he lets me buy something, I feel as though he's approving of me working.'

Other high-earning women may justify themselves because they are supporters of a human cause – an idealistic, unsuccessful husband, perhaps – or give their children greater opportunity, or help ageing parents. So Lorraine is happy to support her artistic husband in his work, which is high on idealism and low on earnings:

'He is not ambitious in the way I am. He wants to create beautiful things, and he earns a lot less than I do. I feel I'm investing some of my money in his talent, which could be important. He works just as hard as I do, so there's no feeling on either side that he's spongeing on me. But I do make it possible for him to pursue his own kind of ambition.'

Lorraine believes her money is helping a good cause, and the moral purpose allays guilt. Social psychologist Carol Gilligan has said that women define morality as not hurting others – in morality lies a way of solving conflicts so that no one gets hurt. Their relationship with their money can trigger an internal conflict over their status as 'good' women.

Power

In the Far East, where understanding of the West is almost entirely based on a business relationship, businesswomen are increasingly offered access to the same symbolic signals of power as men. Japan has several clubs providing men for businesswomen. For years, on journalistic assignments in luxury international hotels, I got used to passing the lines of prostitutes at the public telephones in the lobby ringing men's rooms to tout for business. On my most recent business trip, for the first time I was regularly called in my room by young men explicitly offering their services as paid escort. And a colleague, long used to men's attempts to pick her up when she was away on business, was astonished recently to be approached by a young man who named his price for spending the night with her. 'He was beautifully dressed. Obviously business was good for him,' she said.

This kind of thing is a misreading of the shifts in power in Western business culture. Sarah says:

> 'One of the things that used to exclude women from senior management was being expected to entertain male clients with those awful messy nights out. Thank God that's changed. To a woman, it was just a waste of good money.
>
> 'Recently two of my executives were away on business, and they found women had been procured for them. They both separately made excuses and rang me up in the middle of the night asking what on earth they could do to get out of it.'

It may be that there are now enough women making their more open, more altruistic management approach felt even in the secretive financial underbelly of traditional masculine business practice. Or the material rewards women reap from their success at work are not necessarily important in comparison with the satisfactions of openness and consensus. Those are the achievements which bring women confidence.

At work, money could be seen as the source of these

women's power to serve the moral purpose by putting into practice their various visions of what business should be about. Suzanne says:

'There's a difference in the way I deal with public money – the business profits or losses. I find that actually the old concept of femininity still applies there – you know, balancing the housekeeping budget. I suppose there may be a hangover from seeing my mother manage the family budget which makes me ultra-careful, and very cautious about taking any risks. I feel very aware that if you can't fund expansion or whatever, it makes things miserable for the people involved. I'd rather look after the people I've got than risk their livelihoods, even though new people might benefit.

'Private money is different. It's my very own. I've paid for it, and I can do what I like with it. On the other hand, because I know the price I paid for it, I don't treat it lightly. Though sometimes I find I swing towards wild extravagance, when I buy things I don't even really want to prove I can. I usually do that before Christmas, or buying birthday presents, so people will know I've got it to spend. And then I don't buy anything for ages. I go to the office in trousers sometimes because I've only got laddered tights, and I resent having to keep replacing them.'

Money: Security

Ellen savours the money she earns for the security it guarantees:

'I call it security, but it's more than that. I could be secure on a much smaller salary than I get, but it matters that there's a lot of it. It's the difference between being independent and being really free. It gives me the power to control my own life, not just exist. It's not that I actually do anything with the money to demonstrate that, but I know I have it. Actually, I think the women who go in for a lot of show – huge houses, swimming pools, and lots of jewellery – are not women who earn it because they're successful in business. They're the women who marry rich men, and they buy things like that to show some man loves them enough to give them the money to do it. That's pathetic.'

Young and Monied

High-earning younger women's attitudes to having money of their own are changing. Most of them have been brought up by a generation of women who earned money themselves from work, even if they saw it as pin money. Joan watches her sons' girlfriends, who are all studying for careers:

'They have been protected and insulated by the sacrifices of my generation of working women. They saw their mothers working. Their mothers gave them money. But older women were asked for – and felt they had to give – gratitude. These girls don't have any sense of service or responsibility when it comes to money, any sense of it being put to good use. They use it to gratify what they want. We're going to be dependent on these toughies for support in our old age.'

A successful young woman like Lisa, though, accepts all her money as her due:

'I am good at what I do. I work hard. I earn the money. If people have a problem with that, it's their problem. There's some sort of convention among a lot of older women that we should be ashamed of earning large amounts of money. I think it's envy – not necessarily of the money, but the things money represents, like freedom and independence and not having to give a damn if other people like you or not.'

Here, Lisa acknowledges an element of fear which colours women's attitudes to money. Traditionally, women 'earned' money by being loveable. They still often tend to equate having money with being loved. Now that they are earning their own money, there is a real fear that they have cut themselves off from the proof that they are loved. It is a fraught subject. Few women boast about the amount they have, yet more women than ever before have considerable spending power. Women are not only earning their own money regardles of men's support, but through successful careers they have access to occupational pensions; they will probably inherit from parents who owned their own property.

Sheila, as a finance director earning 'a lot of money', is unusual in seeing money as a liberating element:

'I am closer to my innate character than I have ever been. I can do a lot of things I used to feel I couldn't – put up a different point of view, ask about something I don't understand, admit I'm wrong.'

Nothing there about what her money can buy – she values it for the confidence it brings her to be herself. Perhaps that gives some idea of how such women, as economic dependants, had to distort their personalities to conform to acceptable female convention.

Fear

Frances Lear, who launched the American magazine *Lear's* and is a very rich woman in her own right, says:

> 'My fear of managing money I've made from previous life's work comes from my not being able to make it again. I could make other money, but not that old money again. The difference between those who make money and those who inherit it is that the latter are so remote from their money and they have no confidence in their own relationship to it. And therefore they're terrified of the people who manage it for them because they don't have any idea how it was made in the first place.'

Andrea understands only too well the terror associated with money. When she first set up her business, she came very close to failure:

> 'I was horribly in debt in my first four years. I was very frightened. I went to my ex-husband, who was a great help in the initial stages, and to a friend who had been unemployed. My husband said I must liquidate. I said I can't, because I couldn't pay everyone. He said I'd only got limited liability of £1,000, and I must liquidate. I felt total responsibility for other people. You see how hard they work. If someone doesn't pay you, you physically can't pay them, but as long as you're afloat, you've got to keep baling. I got out of the spiral by a stroke of good fortune – but how far are you responsible for your own luck?
>
> 'I made a vow that when I got out of debt, I'd never get

into it again. The trouble is you think too small. But I'm not frightened now of spending money as long as I know what I'm spending it for. I know now that I have to look for trouble, and that I can cope with it. You can't learn that from just being told.

'You gain a lot of confidence and feminine pride, you know, once you have proved you are still a contender and you won through by doing what you think was the right thing by the people who depend on you.'

Andrea admits that her business nearly failed because of her ignorance about what making her own money involved:

'I started the business after a conversation with a woman friend on a beach. She asked me what I wanted more than anything else, and I said money. We sort of took it on from there, with me thinking I'd get paid lots of loot for a good idea, and then be a kind of adviser on a huge salary while other people did the rest. But I'd no idea what was involved. For the first four years I was in debt. It was terrible. I was so frightened. I didn't even know about books and audits. The accountant asked what my stock was worth. I'd no idea. My acountants' bill was bigger than turnover.

'I get people writing to say they liked my products, or to complain. The way they write is interesting: full of suspicion, mistrust, thinking everyone is out to cheat them. People who don't have enough to do look for trouble and find it. That was me before I worked. One of the things that earning my own money has taught me is great sympathy for the predicament of men. I feel really sorry for my ex-husband. The idea that you're the breadwinner, and most women simply don't understand what things cost. It's because the husband wants control of the money, as mine did; it becomes an uncomfortable game. I thought he was fussy; he thought I was a spendthrift because I lost bills. I see now what comes from not being in control.'

Andrea is not alone in finding the financial rites of passage between economic dependence and independence painful. There is already a booming demand for money therapy, ranging from person-to-person money advice to specialist psychiatrists. Such a specialist practising in the United States says:

'Perhaps the biggest boom in money therapy is coming from women with a fear of making too much money. If financial care is the corollary of love, then financial success can be a threat to femininity.'

Men and Women's Money

Certainly men, too, are having problems dealing with women's new capacity to earn as much or more than they do. A man can feel that his partner's earnings strike at the core of his masculinity. Ellen remembers dealing with a colleague whose husband also worked for the firm:

'She was very good indeed, and was promoted. We have a reward system, and she earned the pay rises she got. But he didn't get them. It was awful. Every time she was promoted, with the higher salary, he would start applying for jobs at the same level or higher – jobs he was never going to get. She began to dread her pay rises. Fortunately, he got a job elsewhere and left. Now that he doesn't see her promotions on the noticeboard, she keeps them quiet.'

Several successful women, who are now divorced, say that their husbands were unable to cope with their success. Money was mentioned every time. Take Sheila:

'When we married I was in my early twenties; he was in his thirties. As my career took off, he had a problem. He was brought up traditionally, and thought he should be earning more. I could have given it up for him, but then I wouldn't have been the person I am, and I don't think you can live your life that way. Equally, he couldn't come to terms with it.'

A male-dominated system can also make it difficult for women to convince money men to take them seriously as businesswomen. For Dounne the problem of getting bank managers to take her business seriously is compounded by the fact that she is black. She says there are specific problems for black women:

'Black British businesses are classified as ethnics; hence they lack status, respect, recognition and economic wealth. I believe the only way forward is to escape from the poverty trap of dependence on men.'

She quotes a 1990 survey by Professor Ellis Cashmore of Aston Business School in Birmingham: 'On average a third of the black and Asian people setting up companies are women, which is roughly the same figure as whites.' In the light of that, and of her own experience, she is very disparaging about the masculine-biased banking system's attitude to women:

'I'd got orders from chains of supermarkets, including Safeway and Tesco, for my product, and I needed to expand into factory premises to cope with demand. I needed an overdraft to buy raw materials and hire an automatic filling and capping machine. The bank manager was well aware that if I could not guarantee continuous supplies to these companies, I might be delisted, and the business ruined. He told me I should have stayed small, and why didn't I take my products to a large manufacturer and pay them to make them for me? I'd won the national Women Mean Business competition run by the BBC, too. It made no difference. The bank would not help me beyond the government's Loan Scheme. He advised me to see a lawyer about the possibilities of liquidation, in case the bank called in the loan. At first sight this may look like racism, but it's happening to black and white businesswomen alike.'

Looking Monied

Women's relationship with money is more complex than men's. Women who earn a lot by their own success at work challenge the traditional balance of power between men and women. They also have to come to terms with the demands money makes on them. Money is far more than lifeless coinage; its power goes well beyond simple buying and selling. It has to be put to use if it is to retain its power to get results. This applies on a very basic level – if you leave it alone, the realities of economic life, inflation, and so on, mean that it will lose value. Invest it, and something will happen – it will change in value. Whether it goes up or down depends on the quality of your decision on how to invest it.

Women's experience of decision-making over money is usually learned from the use they see their mothers make of it in the household budget. They spend on caring for the family. A good mother puts herself last. Spending on herself is usually fraught with guilt – with the feeling that the money spent on replacing her worn-out coat is spent to the disadvantage of her children. Even for women who are well used to making tough business decisions, there is a moral dimension to spending money which complicates the issue enormously.

Successful women have to reinvest some of their earnings

in maintaining their business persona. They may not like what they have to spend on. The feminist barrister Anna Coote went to court to win recognition that her working clothes – in her case, legal black – were tax-deductible as business equipment, not her choice of clothes. The fact that she lost does not invalidate the way she and many others feel. Chief executive Sarah promises herself:

'When I retire I'll be the scruffiest so-and-so. I do notice that from the time when I was first a director, on board meeting days I'm very careful about how I dress. The amount of money I've spent makes me feel secure that I look right.'

Why do women in senior management gain confidence by spending money on clothes they would not wear in other areas of their lives? Suzanne says:

'I don't know why I should dislike the clothes and not the job. It doesn't make sense. Perhaps part of my satisfaction from the job is to feel I'm working to change things for the better, and having to wear the clothes is a reminder I'm still under the cosh.

'It's the same for men. They change their suits more often these days, and they don't smell. In a sense, they've come to meet women on neutral ground. I think perhaps men and women are presenting themselves in a way that can't be categorised by gender.'

A Better World?

Women see the 'applied' function of money as important. Many want to use money to bring about a better world for everyone, not as an end in itself. Sheila, as a finance director, thinks that women bring a moral dimension to their relationship with profit. Most successful women look on their company's profit as a means of maintaining their female vision of management as working for the good of all the people who are part of the business. Janet says:

'The men who'd been running the company had been inept. They didn't think you could be overstaffed. The business was going down the drain. When I took over, I knew it was a question of dealing with profit and the bottom line versus the human side. They thought I was extremely ruthless. We couldn't support the numbers of people. They had to be fired. I rationalised it by saying it was to protect the company – i.e. the people. They couldn't see that company survival depends on profitability.'

The classic example of the profit motive based deliberately on an ethical cause is the Body Shop. Anita Roddick has been accused of putting money into projects that may have high social priority but are not necessarily in the best interests of the shareholders. She retorts: 'Our financial responsibility is to keep the moral fabric of the company flourishing.'

Maybe capitalism itself is the fundamental problem for women. The ambitious women who seek to bring about a better work environment, a better company, a better world for all through their business success, can do so only by adopting the opposing principles of capitalism. Their work is also the only arena for experimenting with a moral compromise on this. Religion once offered a possible route, but today's successful women often feel alienated from traditional religions, whose way of interpreting the female role in society is quite irrelevant to the realities of ambitious women's lives. These women are left with their work to provide them with a spiritual and moral framework. They say that the ethical priority of a capitalist business need not conflict with the best interests of shareholders. Sarah believes 'a business must be run within the ethics of business'. That means:

'I don't find decision-making hard because to me my job is to maximise the profits for the shareholders, not to make Sarah more clever, or the company the best-known brand in the business. What the company is there for is to make a profit for shareholders. If you show your management team that you're not after kudos or self-aggrandisement, you're making the business profitable, then the rest follows.'

Joan found that other people's preconceptions about money present a barrier to communication which can drive people apart:

'It is a kind of language, a form of communication, or misunderstanding. I wanted to create a business to help people sort out the problems between them, and that meant it had to be profitable. I started it because I felt there was a need, which presupposes that people would pay for my services. Otherwise, there's no business. I always intended to help other people. I started out to raise funds for a housing trust. The organisation as I came into it was a bureaucracy running the property they'd bought. I set out to exploit capitalism for a socialist purpose, if you like. There is always a conflict – even on the basic level that housing should be run by local authorities and not a voluntary non-representational body. It was a very political situation, but I'm quick on my feet and don't take offence easily. I had to handle Kensington toffs as well as Rastas. It was an advantage being a woman rather than a man in some areas. It was always me who'd stand and scream at them. I didn't fit the female role they were expecting. To prevent violence I'd engineer a screaming tantrum. It was quite calculated. We sent out women rent collectors because the black community wouldn't attack them. We had to have the money to make the scheme work for everyone.'

Joan went into housing, a field where her business aims can be closely allied to care. For women like Lorraine, though, there has to be a self-interested competitive edge to spice profit, even though the purpose of profit is to promote a happy and productive workplace:

'My own mother left university when she had me and has done significant voluntary work rather than a paid career. It's a bit like the women's ghetto, though, where success not achieved in the open workplace is somehow second-rate. Somehow, if the profit isn't part of standards of professional efficiency, they're not mainstreamers.'

Business management practice has now moved into many areas where previously it played no part – community housing, for example, or schools. Here profit is measured not in money but in value for money, and the quality of the product 'bought'. The monetary profit motive plays a much smaller role in management success for Karen, who now runs her school's budget as part of her job as head:

'Society doesn't encourage women like me to see themselves as skilled managers, but I have got a lot of management skills which apply to any business. When I'm asked what I do for a living, I sometimes say I run a small business for a local authority. Essentially that's what it is. It's not profit-led. The style is altruistic. There's no profit motive in education, but the idea of team-building and being effective in relations with people is very difficult within the male management model. There's a political side to it. Management style is intended to open up schools, but parents, in my experience, are interested in discipline, school uniform and dinners. Beyond that they don't give a damn, and think it's a closed world. We get ten parents out of six hundred coming to open evenings, and it hurts.'

Most successful women in mainstream business, though, feel that profitability and the good of the community – the company community, or the local or national community at large – depend on one another. Here, too, there are signs of a shift in traditional masculine attitudes. Robert Evans, chairman and chief executive of British Gas, wrote recently that business has discovered links between community prosperity and company profitability. Four hundred top British companies have now joined Business in the Community and, in spite of recession, see community involvement as a long-term investment.

Does the fact that it is a man saying this suggest that the money Establishment may be undergoing the same kind of radical shift towards new priorities as we are seeing in the business culture as a whole? Sarah has noticed a different attitude over the last two years:

'I go to the City now and every other banker is female, as are the analysts. It makes what was a very male atmosphere far less daunting, because they're just ordinary folk and easier to deal with. It's a myth that they're strident, hard-faced women. I don't meet any women like that – only in the academic world, which is full of them.'

If women are changing the atmosphere at the centre of financial power, and we have established that some women see a moral purpose to profit, it cannot be a coincidence that the growth in women's monetary clout mirrors growing institutional interest in ethical investment. The most concrete success here was in the economic campaign against apartheid, when pressure from investors forced Barclays Bank to move out of South Africa. On a broader scale, too, the manipulation of investment is affecting various companies' policy in line with 'feminine' priorities. Companies accused of pollution find their creditworthiness as damned as they would if they had corporate convictions for fraud.

Money: Politics

At the same time, company contributions to the political parties are falling off. This goes hand in hand with a growing lack of interest in party politics and the process of Parliament among change-agent women. It seems likely that for women, control over money is replacing the right to vote as a means of making change in the administration of the country. Women won the right to vote, and it did not give them an equal voice in government. But as they take an increasingly significant hold over the getting and spending of money, they have prospects of real power. Conservative Treasury Minister Gillian Shephard says:

'Many successful women see Parliament as almost academic. Young women I talk to say there's no point in considering it as a career. There's the hours, but mainly they can't see the point. Legislation helping women is perceived to have come from Europe, and they feel they can achieve more from outside Parliament. I think the way Westminster is run is a very foolish way to live for both men and women. There's no need for so much of the nonsense. Other countries don't run it in this way. But I do feel some interplay is important between politics and business.'

Most successful women are political in that their management aims involve improving the lot of a wider community than their own self-interest. They show little confidence in an existing political system which has proved itself ineffectual as a means of bringing this about. Some see it as damaging to a business community which needs stability. It seems that for women at this level, both Labour and Conservative parties are implicated in a male-dominated business culture. If they are trying to adapt to the new feminisation, they still lag well behind the reality of the change. The question is whether the existing system actually depends for its survival on continuing failure to adapt to that reality. Janet says:

> 'I've always had problems working for capitalistic success and socialistic principles at the same time. I do now declare that I'm a Labour supporter – once I wouldn't have dared. I believe you can be a socialist and run your own company. From within the Party, I can try to change the policy of public ownership, which I abhor. I loathe institutional investors investing in my business. I like performance-related business, so I disagree with Labour opposition to that.'

This suggests a new political departure for some women – an assertive intention to change party policy rather than let party policy stifle feminine initiatives. It is significant that the women who have the power to try to force the pace should be women in business. Theirs is now more than a token force to be reckoned with. Women's access to the financial clout which wields this kind of power is very recent, nor can it now be taken away.

The psychologist Harmon, in her 1970 study of female managers, found that learning to drive a car and an urban or farming background were important factors in the making of senior businesswomen.

A woman learning to drive a car as soon as she legally can demonstrates, it seems, a drive to take control of her environment and step away from male control. Certainly all our sample drive cars. Cars, indeed, were mentioned often as one of the best perks of business success. Annie, a public-relations consultant, takes the car as a control symbol even further. When she drives up to the luxury Mayfair hotels which are often her business venues, the doorman usually refuses to park her car. She simply leaves it in the street with the keys inside. They always park it.

The urban or agricultural background, according to this study, imbues a strong drive to get out and away for social and academic achievement. As we have seen, financial director Sheila was brought up in a close-knit mining community in Derbyshire. Several of my interviewees were brought up in large cities. It may be significant that the least driven to succeed in terms of power and influence is Anne, whose roots are in a small provincial town: 'I get a kick out of being seen to have things, because I get respect for that.'

If – as it would seem from these women's capacity to project themselves into an image that pleases others – successful women no longer believe that what they feel is the same thing as what they think, they have indeed grown beyond the old-fashioned concept of femininity. The understanding of the difference could actually be a definition of growing up. In that case, successful businesswomen can at last claim to be fully adult.

6

PRIVATE LIVES

Love Is . . .

Happy and successful career women might think twice before agreeing that the world is well lost for love; but that doesn't mean they don't want love to make their world go round.

In fact, to judge by the women I talked to, they know what they're talking about. They all, when young, launched themselves on the wings of love in marriage or long-term partnerships, and all but two came down to earth with a bang. Those two are still married to their original co-skypilots. But one of them, Joan, did not marry until well into her thirties. The other, Lorraine, admits that her marriage went through a very rocky patch until their son was born eighteen months ago.

Except for two – Sarah and Sheila – they are all now happy in second-time-round relationships, and they put

159

this down to taking certain lessons to heart. For my successful women, what Tolstoy said of happy families is true of happy marriage: 'All happy marriages are alike, but an unhappy marriage is unhappy after its own fashion.' Second time round, they'd learned to weigh their options; they costed the job; and then there's the bottom line – what shall it profit the woman?

Lorraine, for instance, argues:

> 'Successful women have to choose a husband to support them. They don't need financial support, or to be looked after. What they need is respect and encouragement, not competition. That means a man who won't kill to get to the top himself. Now a bit of me is attracted to that kind of man, but it would be impossible for me to live with him and do what I do. Some senior executive girl-friends and I were chatting among ourselves recently, and we realised that of the married ones who were still married, all the husbands were not very successful.'

Because they have a very high degree of job satisfaction, and love their work, these women are not looking to enter the relationship to improve a bad situation. Dare I suggest that in a real sense they marry for love because they are already happy? They do not need to see husbands as potential breadwinners, or look on men as protectors. They see them as lovers, companions and partners. The early feminists all knew that economic independence was the only real way to liberate women. Successful women now approach their relationships with the knowledge that all other things are equal. They are as well-paid, as well-educated, as skilled and as successful as their male equivalents. They also take it for granted that because of their work, their lives are fast-moving and subject to swift and complete change.

But they do want to be couples or families. Sheila would certainly marry again if she met the right man; Sarah has mentioned elsewhere that she is lonely outside work without a relationship.

The relationships they want, however, are different. They want to be equal partners with their own discrete identity, not complementary sides to a single persona, the couple. Nevertheless, their domestic lives as such are more narrowly defined than most women's. These women do not clean their own homes. They have nannies to look after their children. They have all the labour-saving devices available. If they have pets, they have cats or fish, not dogs. Their priorities, duties and demands are laid down in unwritten contract – sometimes it is even written! But first they have talked about it. Lorraine says that she and her husband meet at the start of every week to negotiate over who covers for the nanny on her night off: 'I may have to go to the City; he may have a meeting. We decide which is the most important, which can be rescheduled.' The distinction between private and public life is almost gone.

Expectations

It has been said that the relationships in our society that we think are about love are really about power. Feminine women are supposed to define themselves as very loving, because in that lies their 'power'. But highly ambitious women have rejected that kind of love with their drive for – and achievement of – a different kind of power, a different definition of womanhood. The balance of authority in their relationships is utterly changed.

Does this mean that their relationships are based on a different – better – kind of loving?

It is curious that the drive and ambition which make these women different from others are almost always fostered in the context of what they see as the source of their lack of difference – a background strong on the emotional bond of family. All my interviewees took it for granted initially that they would marry and have children. Whatever the circumstances which initially coloured their expectations from relationships with other people – from single parent to widowed mother, from parents absent overseas to religious convention – most successful women feel strong ties to relatives and old friends. Yet their adult relationships very often seem to lack the trappings of that kind of emotional bond. Rather, they are higher on rationale. Has love become, like money, something to be kept to themselves?

In the business context, according to Michael, marriage has traditionally been looked on as positive for men, negative for women. But he thinks that the masculine-biased culture in multinationals is changing on this issue:

'These days women expect to have children and a serious career as a right. We've had to work very hard on the managers who select for promotion to get rid of the hang-up that women aren't as flexible. They wouldn't ask men about their families. And with returners, it's obvious for them to work part-time, and this has been very slow and frustrating to women. It took a long time to agree at all – the corporate view was that we employ people on a full-time basis, and very few jobs in this company can be done part-time. Therefore we don't want to encourage part-time because if we allow women with babies to do it we will have to allow lots of others, and that would be disastrous. Gradually, though, this has changed, and we have set up a part-time scheme for women, limited to forty places. It's partly out of self-interest, let it be said, because we were losing good people.'

But the old attitude is not dead yet. Lorraine, who advises multinationals on senior executive development, recognises special problems for women because 'they are expected to get married and have children and lose their ambition':

'Life is very hard for women in multinationals. They identify a group of people they think will go to the top. My client has identified 180 people, 10 of them women. Forty per cent of the people available for selection were women, and they chose just 10. Do you wonder more women set up on their own? The system in multinationals has been set up by men for men. If you're ambitious you need to work long hours, and you need to be mobile. I've lived apart from my husband for years at a time because our jobs have led one or other of us to go somewhere else.

'A friend of mine took her family to the US while her husband stayed in Britain, and another woman I know went on a two-week residential management course. Unbeknown to the organisation, she paid for the nanny and kids to stay in a hotel close to the college. As far as her promotion went, her kids were an embarrassment. They were something you do on the side, like an affair.

'The point is, men want to maintain the system, and to do that they feed myths about female priorities.'

Love's Swings and Roundabouts

Societal pressure, particularly outside big cities, still reflects some of this. Society's expectations from marriage were bound to change once a critical mass of women found that the demands of their working lives conflicted directly with their personal lives. This is happening to some degree at all levels of the workplace. In the upper echelons of business and management, women have already absorbed the cultural change.

Since the late sixties, the Pill has not only given women control over their fertility, it has allowed them to reassess what purpose they might serve in society. The reproductive anchor weighed, women were freed to pursue economic independence – either solo, or within a conventional relationship.

It is understandable if many women are afraid of the implications of redefining womanhood. It is natural that they fear a damaging split between those who are eager to move ahead at full throttle, and the many others who are not in a position to do so. After the tremendous struggle for liberation, many women do not want to lose the idea of sisterhood, where the strong protect the weak. But strong and successful women show no sign that they are trying to free themselves from a responsibility to other women. On the contrary, they have shown by their style of management and use of power that they want to open up new opportunities to others. This includes men. Many successful women, watching men at work trying to get in touch with long-suppressed emotional aspects of themselves, would want to help them. Where successful older women saw men as adversaries or enemies, young ones do not. They want balance, not victory.

Their attitudes and expectations are changing what they want from their own personal relationships. Anne's experience, for example, is a microcosm of this process of development from subjugated little girl to independent woman:

'My parents had no expectation that I would go to university. I was convent-educated, and we had one careers discussion in the fifth form. I said I wanted to be a vet. It was like wanting to be a fairy. I wasn't taking the right exams.

'My main idea was to leave home and be independent. I assumed that meant getting married. Anything I did for myself was passing time until I had a family. I married Simon while he was at university, so I worked at various temp jobs to support us for a year.

'After that, it did seem there was an awful lot of the rest of my life. I was encouraged by an Australian woman working with me in a bookshop. She pushed me to university. I always felt far less of a person than Simon because he was educated. I went to university at twenty-seven, and found I'd got a brain. I enjoyed it and did well. Within months of my getting my degree, though, Simon and I were separated. It changed the balance of our relationship. He was supportive while I was at university with financial help, but our sexual relationship faded while I was there. It changed our relationship because it changed my sense of myself. I took myself more seriously and believed myself more capable of serious things.'

Also, the new equality in the balance of marital power is proving difficult for some men. Some are desperately seeking a means of protecting their own security. Often this is why they become involved with a 'strong' woman, but almost invariably they see her success, when it comes, as a threat. Men who cannot adapt to the idea that marriage or partnership between men and women is intrinsically an equal one will cast themselves in the weak and submissive role if the woman refuses to play it. Lucy, who runs her own research business, married Tom, a psychologist:

'He had been married before, but they split up. I had been doing some work for him, and we started an affair and he left his wife for me. At least, that's what I thought, but now I believe they had been separated for some time before we started going out. That's because he started going out with his secretary when she thought we were still together – it was only six months after our son was born, for God's sake, what else was she to think? But actually he'd moved out before the baby was born.

'Tom was great at first. He is a great believer in independent women, and he encouraged – no, he pushed – me into going out to work. He got me bits of work through his academic contacts, and he really taught me how to become a career person.

'I wanted the baby, but he was pleased, too. But that was the end of the marriage. He loves the boy, and sees a lot of him, but now he's moved on to try his Svengali act on the secretary. I feel as though he needs to create a strong self-supporting Mummy figure out of his wife, and when he's done that, he can't bear it that she has a real son and makes him into a Daddy when he wants to be the bloody baby. How's that for male manipulation?'

Joan believes that the numbers of men who find they cannot help reacting in this way will increase as the first significant flush of dedicated career women in their late thirties and forties turn into Silver Goddesses in their fifties:

'These women have had successful careers, they're used to cash, they're educated and still working. I think at that stage they'll see advantages in marrying younger men: sex, companionship and a maternal outlet at a stroke! Particularly since they're the generation which probably did have their careers at the expense of children anyway. The young men will be afraid of their female contemporaries. They'll be trying to get back in touch with the feminine side of themselves which they had to reject to become men, and they will find their salvation in attractive and active older women.'

Sarah, who has never been married, wonders how couples survive when the balance between the daily experiences and stimuli of everyday life are entirely different for husband and wife:

'It's tough when you can't even be natural at home because someone else depends on you to give a point to their day. I have a housekeeper, and in some ways it's like being a man married to a stay-at-home wife. She is the kind of Tory who reads the *Daily Mail*, and I'm really quite liberal on political issues. All her opinions come from what she reads in the paper. I can't argue with her, because of our relative positions. I don't want to come home at the end of a tough day, and have to listen to her views. She's entitled to them, but I don't want to hear them. We eat our meals separately now, which at least puts a formal distance between us, which you couldn't with a wife. But it is a bit daft, two people eating alone in the same house.'

Down Side

Many women have found that in practice men do not believe they meant what they said they wanted out of the relationship, and either bank on a change of heart, or simply can't compete. It is becoming clear that in marriage, as at work, the masculine culture was designed to protect male vulnerability on the emotional front. Janet describes how her first husband was unable to cope with her determination to pursue her career:

'I admit I was driven. My job came first. The reason the marriage broke up was I learned too late that if you are a driven career person you should never, ever, marry anyone you're competitive with because men can't take it. We were in the same trade, at the same level. You'd think it would be lovely to share, but he resented it very much. He worked for one of our clients, and continued to give us business – he was very ambivalent and very unhappy. He wouldn't accept it, wouldn't talk about it. I tried – even went into analysis to try and sort it out. He put it down to me being a hard bitch, not like other women. He said I didn't understand him, was too concerned about business. But he'd married me knowing the person I was. He'd been married to a career woman before, for eighteen months. She couldn't stand it, being held back in case she hurt him. I think in the end what he wanted was someone to push him up the ladder rather than make their own way. He never married again. But now I'd sacrificed something for my career, and it threw me. I blamed myself, and took my eye off the ball professionally.'

If the man does not accept equality, the relationship becomes a struggle for supremacy, with her identity as the prize. That independent identity is too hard-won to relinquish. Sheila describes the process as it happened in her marriage:

'My job is the most important thing in my life – as it would be with a man. I do have a broader life, and it's not the only thing in it, but it is the most important. If you're going to get to a senior position in anything, you're going to have to put the commitment in. If I was married . . .? It's part of the reason for my divorce. We met when I was in my early twenties and he was in his thirties, and as my career took off, he had a problem. He was brought up traditionally, and when I was earning more, doing more, and because he was older, he had a problem. If I were to meet somebody, then my priorities might change – but would be based on me as I am now.'

Sarah's long-term relationship went the same way when she became managing director of her company:

'It went wrong when I got the promotion. He went and applied for a job where he'd be an MD too, and it all went wrong. He should never have been one, and he became competitive with me. If my car got bigger, he'd go to his office and demand a bigger car. I didn't realise it was happening. Whether I changed, I don't know, but we ended up not talking about work at home at all, and it became very false because I'd just talk about anything rather than what was really worrying me.'

Love's Reasons

Lorraine, her only marriage still intact after seven years, argues that ambitious women should choose for relationships men who complement rather than conflict with their careers:

'I actually asked somebody what are the characteristics of successful men, and he said one of the things was, they choose a wife to support them. That's what the smart ones do. I look at myself and friends when we were choosing our men, and there's truth in it. My marriage went through a bad patch when he was working in Europe. We were real Dinkies [Double Income No Kids] – never saw each other, no food in the fridge. I was out of the UK one week a month. One of the offices I managed was in Manchester, so I was there once a week. I've still got my diaries and every now and then I look back. I just worked the whole time, from 8 a.m. to 8 p.m. The men who had families kept them in the country and had flats in town themselves in the week.

'I have a very supportive husband, both emotionally and physically at home. He has never competed with me. I see girls who can't get it together, and they have husbands who don't support them. They put their own jobs first. I've had girl chats to friends of mine who are high-powered executives, and we are all married to men who are not ambitious, and wouldn't kill to get to the top. My husband isn't going to kill to get to the top. Such men, married to powerful women, get the same as a woman married to a powerful man – money. I can earn a huge salary and my husband doesn't, and he's been able to develop his company as he likes on my support.

There's very little difference between how ambitious men and like-minded women do things in a relationship. I get pissed off with people who say that a woman is more sensitive. I'm the least sensitive of my colleagues here, and the toughest.'

Janet, too, found that her second marriage is founded on her husband's comparative lack of ambition:

'My present husband is not in the same business as me. He has no ambition. He could have done so much, but he never stretched himself. I can talk to him. He's not the most insightful person, but he's very good company. There's no competition between us – though there is between business and home for me. When I put business first, my husband isn't an angel. He makes it clear he thinks it's terrible. Most evenings I'm tied up with business, and I feel guilty. But when the crunch comes, business comes first. It has to. I do feel guilty. He had a birthday yesterday and I'm aware I should be spending more time with him – but then women feel guilty about everything.'

Sally, on the other hand, puts the success of her second marriage down to genuine career equality:

'I do think we have achieved that. I've noticed that if I move ahead on the salary scale, he's not far behind. He could soar ahead and it wouldn't bother me. He is very successful. Women at senior levels are quite isolated, and if I need someone to talk to, I take it home. If I'm stressed, instead of bottling it up, which I used to do, I go home and shout at the cat – or him. I get tremendous emotional support from him.'

It seems that relationships with men play a very important part in career women's lives. Their job satisfaction means they can still be happy without – or between – such a relationship, but their expectations as women now involve both as complementary aspects of fulfilment. And in the successful cases I've quoted, the men concerned have been happy to accept the women's terms. This is a huge step beyond the old assumption – by men and many women – that a woman's success is defined by the priority of being a good wife and mother, whatever little job she may do on the side. It also makes it more difficult to define what is involved for a successful career woman in being a good wife. Helena Kennedy, successful barrister who took silk, defines herself as the 'managing director of my family'. Lorraine says:

'I do think having kids is really the crunch. Having a child completely changed our relationship. We have to negotiate about how we organise it now. The world of business is set up by men for men, and if you work for a multinational and you're ambitious, you need to work long hours and be mobile. It's almost impossible for a woman with children to do that.'

Children: To Have Or Not to Have?

The question of children is crucial – if, and when? The average age for women having their first child has risen from twenty to twenty-four in the mid 1970s to twenty-five to twenty-nine now, which seems to support my impression that successful career women tend to put off motherhood until they are well enough established at work to be able to continue with their careers. Certainly, the women I talked to who are under forty had faced the question of whether or not to have children as a decision to be made, rather than something that happened automatically. Here again, this may seem unsentimental, but that is not the way they see it. It is simply another aspect of the control over their lives they have gained from success.

At the same time, this is the area of the business culture most resistant to female priorities. Lisa, for example, says:

'There's a sort of sexism I don't want to get involved with at the top of the company. It would be very difficult for me to be managing director. I'd like to be, but with a child I couldn't put in the extent of commitment they want, while a man is prepared to sacrifice his family for the job. It isn't that he doesn't have to sacrifice his family, you understand. He's willing to. I don't think anyone should be expected to sacrifice family for career. It's unnecessary, but it's part of the macho rules about how we do business. I think the working practice is wrong. But though I'd like to be managing director, and believe I could do it, I don't think it will happen now I've got a family.'

Many successful women agonise over the decision to have children because having a child can change the careful gender balance in their relationship as well as at work.

For some, the problem is comparatively simple. They question whether the innate maternal instinct is as dispensable as a feminine *sine qua non* as was the rest of the claptrap imposed on women. And here there is a profound division between women who do and women who don't. An EC survey of women in Germany in 1988 found that 10 per cent of working women do not want to have children. Sheila says:

'There are still pressures for women because of society's expectations. I made a choice, based on my natural inclination. I'm not maternal. I haven't tried not to be. I love travelling, and friends outside the business. I think a lot of women get so far up the ladder and then decide not to pursue further promotion. That may be the moment they decide to have a child, to give themselves a reason for stopping. They have to make choices, and choices take them in different directions. They try to be Superwoman and find it's not on and something has to go, and by then it probably has to be career rather than anything else, once they have children.'

Sally – early divorce, now married again, managing director of a training company – came to a decision with her husband that they would not have children. She wonders if having a child is a cop-out for some career women:

'I believe children blight ambition. We have decided not to have any. It has taken a long time to make a final decision, but we don't need children. Having children is a problem for senior women. They have the choice of being absentee mothers or not having them. It's one of the biggest barriers to progress. I read somewhere that in the back of women's minds is the thought that their job is not all that important because if they don't work they can have a family. I wonder if that's strictly true, and women do see having children as a cop-out. Certainly those who have kids and no career resent those who have careers and no kids. Not the other way round. Mothers miss out on the goodies of a career – power and money.'

And Ellen, who has also decided not to have children, says that, speaking as a boss, she cannot help seeing that for a woman to have children at the start of her career shows a lack of commitment which penalises her chances of promotion. She does not necessarily approve of this, but in the context of her working life today, she thinks it is a fact of life.

Valerie, whose work involves a lot of counselling, has noticed that this issue of career and/or children can make redundancy more difficult for women:

'So much of a person's identity is tied up in work that redundancy is failure. Women certainly see it as such. The rejection of *me* comes out far more strongly for women, so the cut goes deeper. It also often exposes other issues, like having children. The woman is often debating whether to have children, and when she's fired, the husband says now's the time to have kids, but she sees it as a cop-out. So all the issues of redundancy counselling about does she go back to work focus on his wanting her to have a child. She may have intended to, but because it's forced on her, she doesn't want to do it.'

A Question of Attitudes

This suggests that the business culture has moved very little on this particular issue, but none the less, successful women's attitudes have changed considerably. For an older woman, reproduction was part of the feminine convention, and even if her self-esteem did not depend on being a wife and mother, she might feel she had to have children to prove her femininity. If she did not, she could well be marginalised in any social context outside work. Other women – and men – might ask what right she had to hold, let alone express, a view when she had not qualified to speak as a woman. Nor was her opinion worth hearing on 'male' issues, because even if she was well placed in men's world, she was not a man.

My older interviewees' husbands were also more likely to take it for granted that they would have children. Indeed, they often saw fatherhood as a demonstration of their masculinity. Younger men are more likely not to take children for granted. They negotiate. Sally, in her early thirties, says that if her husband had wanted a child, she would have had one.

To Andrea, who started her own company and went to work only when her children had grown up and left home, or to Joan, who organised her property management business so that she was at home when her children came home from school, Sally's attitude sounds clinical. Lisa, now working part-time while her daughter is very young, is considering setting up on her own if the system at work conflicts with motherhood. Anne, too, has given up her job as a senior manager to freelance because that allows her to be both mother and career woman. The corporate system has not yet adjusted to the maternal responsibilities of its high-flying women – and not always on account of male chauvinism.

Younger women may wonder why they often feel constrained to hide the fact that they are mothers at work. The reason is obvious enough with old-fashioned male bosses, who judge all women by their non-working wives and believe, with them, that a mother's place is in the home. That's the choice those wives made, and if they have ever had doubts about their own choice, they can scarcely voice them now and continue to lead their lives. So they support their husbands' ingrained preference for male-only senior management by agreeing that mothers should not have careers. Even so, the attitude of Janet's bosses in the sixties would not be legal now:

'I decided to get pregnant and intended to come back to the same job, as managing director of a subsidiary group. But the main board decided I'd have to take a 10 per cent salary cut, and return as a director, but not managing director.'

Recent articles in influential and opinion-forming newspapers, including *The Times*, about women executives with children make one wonder if there is not some sort of regressive conspiracy afoot to replace men and the male system as the perceived limitation on women's progress. Children and childcare are now put forward as the barrier women have to overcome, the open invitation to look for excuses not to pursue career ambitions – just as women in large numbers are proving themselves highly successful. Ms Jo Cutmore, head of her own recruitment agency and mother of three children under eight, organises meetings for executive women with children. She is quoted as saying: 'I wanted to start a group where we could speak frankly – not necessarily about problems.' And a group member added: 'I don't need to cry on anyone's shoulder . . . I've got better things to do than moan.' Such comments reveal that these women are aware of the implicit threat in the way they are being represented to the public. There is a danger that because of political engineering, the way the new definitions of femininity these women are promoting develop may actually fall short of the reality of what women can achieve. There's still a hint of the old alibi for failure, even when the women under public scrutiny have already proved themselves successful – and even when they repudiate such a professional safety-net. There still appears to be some political percentage for women as a whole to be gained from questioning whether female success can be achieved without an either/or choice between career and a fulfilling relationship.

But what of the attitude of many established career women towards female colleagues who have children? Janet says:

'As a mother employing senior women, I think working life is diluted by kids. I deprecate using children to excuse being unprofessional – and professional means children are not there. Motherhood creates amateurs and dilettantes, and some women resent that because it damages them once they've had children.'

Jo Cutmore, for example, felt that she had to conceal her pregnancies from clients until the ninth month, and took off only the equivalent of a long weekend to get over the births. Only last year, the Equal Opportunities Commission took up the case of businesswoman Mrs Geraldine Hammersley, who tried to take her baby into a training exhibition at the National Exhibition Centre. The organisers refused her entry with the child because, she was told, she was acting unprofessionally, and 'the other exhibitors wouldn't like it'. In that, the organisers were probably right. Anne, former senior manager, says:

'Before I had the baby, I didn't know if I wanted to go back to work. I had a suspicion I'd find it difficult. Once I was pregnant I sort of dismissed myself from the running, and set the tone for them dismissing me. I tried to negotiate a contract with another employer, but they were unwilling. I didn't mention I was pregnant. I certainly kept my personal life out of it. I was negotiating with a woman without children and I wondered if she would regard it as a handicap.'

Sarah finds that in spite of herself, she does:

'It's nothing to do with not liking children. I do like them. I was brought up expecting to have them, and I wanted that. It just hasn't happened, and now I don't miss it. No one can have everything, and that's just one of things that didn't happen for me.

'But speaking as a boss, one of the things I've found difficult working with women is the baby syndrome. Everyone should have a choice, and up to a certain level leaving or maternity leave are no problem. But I have a couple of senior directors who've taken maternity leave in the last three years, and it's really dreadful. One was in a creative job, involving a future range, and we couldn't replace her. She had a lousy pregnancy, so we had a year of her out or one under par. In the end I doubled up, and did it badly. I admit my sympathy was tested. Her job involves travel, and after the baby it had to be left at home and it was traumatic and she's torn. I'm now saying we'll have meetings at 10 a.m. in London instead of earlier somewhere else because I know she wants to be home. I'm still making allowances for her, even without her knowing, and it's not easy. It's seriously affecting the business. If she got pregnant again, I don't know . . . We'd have to have a long talk about it.

'The trouble is, senior women are now having babies at thirty-six when they're in key positions. If I'd had a baby in my thirties, I wouldn't be where I am now at forty, and I wouldn't expect to be. But there is an expectation that you should be. I really don't think I would do both.

'I also think it's not on to bring kids into the office. I've found this quite hard to cope with – the assumption that you'll make the concession because you're a woman. Some women here have two or three children and you'd never notice. It's important when it affects the business and the

woman as professional. There's definitely a shift of emphasis after having a baby. I've never not seen it.

'I think we went through a phase in the eighties when
everyone thought we should all have everything. You can't
have everything, but there's no point in crying over what
didn't happen. People get greedy emotionally and
materially. Those people are still there, and they're moving
through the system.'

Enemies of Promise?

Does Sarah's attitude stem from fear that ambitious and
brilliant women are less likely to fulfil their promise if they
have children? Michael, too, gets the impression that women
lose their motivation to succeed in business once they have
children:

'I'm talking about ambition seen in terms of status in the
hierarchy as opposed to doing a job one really enjoys. I
think a woman is less likely to want to advance into
something she may like less beyond just doing well a job
she enjoys. And from my observation over the years in
personnel, I do think women's ambition changes after
having children. We have a number of women in the
company who at an earlier age were high-fliers, and then
when I check later what happened to them, I find they have
not fulfilled that promise. They charged ahead, and then
stopped. What happened was babies.'

Up to a point, Lorraine thinks:

'I was always very ambitious, as long as I remember. I'm
less so now [after having the child] – which I'm pleased
about. I've been an overachiever for years. I worked my

way up a management consultancy group over seven years. I'm very good at selling consulting. My profession is psychologist, and I'm a good one. I couldn't see any way of having a family and doing the job I was doing. I just worked the whole time.

'With the stress of work, I couldn't conceive. Also I knew I didn't want to stay there for ever. So I moved, and within a year I was pregnant. I teach, and have a consultancy practice where I earn considerably more than before, which was a great deal. I can take lots of time off. I've got it the way I want it. I can say I won't be at meetings till 10 a.m. or after 5 p.m. If they need more, I work weekends. But I'm easier to work with now. I think I was very difficult to live with before I had the child.

'I think it's my right to be a mother and have a job on my terms. I was working in the US at the beginning of the year, when my son was still under a year old, and I took him with me. I was breastfeeding, and I left my husband in Manhattan and took the baby on a work trip with me. On the plane back, we sat next to an incredible woman. Everyone else was pretending I wasn't there, and she asked if she could hold the baby. She had been a partner in a management consultancy group known the world over for being very discriminatory against women – and she had become a partner. She must have been phenomenal. Now she had her own consultancy group employing twenty people. She commuted between New York and Cleveland – a two-hour flight each way. She lived with a bigshot lawyer in New York, and she did it because she was still breastfeeding her son. She was running an incredible business and still breastfed her son. That was her right. I thought that was brilliant. She didn't have to breastfeed, but it was her right to do what she wanted. There would be loads of women who would say why was she making so much fuss out of it?

'At my previous job, one of the projects I worked for was a crèche. The people most against it were the senior women. They didn't have children. They never actually said why should we, but that was the implication.'

Career Plus Motherhood

For Lorraine – as for Lisa and Anne, Joan and Andrea – any tempering of ambition to reach the top has been more than compensated for by the joys of having a child. Lisa, who is thirty, thinks there is a dog-in-the-manger attitude involved in many successful older women's resentment of younger women who combine career success with motherhood. She puts it down to sour grapes.

In practice, though, few childless older businesswomen show any sign at all of feeling bitter or deprived. Not one expressed regrets, or wondered if she had made the right choice in deciding not to have children. Those who did have children admitted that they had probably been poor mothers because although their children had had advantages like good schools and secure lifestyles, these women had usually put business first. Nevertheless, they did not regret having their children. Although in my sample almost all the older women with children were divorced from the fathers, they were unanimous that their children had enormously enriched their lives. But some admit they do not understand why younger women who continue to work full-time after they have children 'bothered' to become mothers. Joan says:

'I ran my own business and arranged my own hours so that I always worked part-time when the children were at home.

I dread to think what will happen with the present generation of young working mothers, who work all hours, and the children just come home to be on their own. I always wanted there to be communication between the children and me. I can't see there's much contact with children now, and I wonder what kind of people today's children will grow up to be.'

I have said that the corporate culture still compartmentalises children and career. Younger women say they feel constrained not to talk about their children at work; we have seen that they feel they must hide pregnancies from clients and employers if they can. 'You're afraid to admit you're a mother. Non-working women see you as not a proper mother, and you're not encouraged to talk about the kids at work,' said one woman. And it is often female colleagues who bring this about. Why?

The first women who broke through the chauvinist barriers to become successful in a male-dominated business world operated in a system where all the industrial legislation distinguished between men as opposed to women-and-chiidren. Children were the lowest common denominator of weakness and dependence, and women took that same status by association. Of course, ambitious women, in fighting for equal status with men, had to dissociate themselves from such criteria of competence or function.

Part of the thrust of such pioneering women was the drive to establish their own unique identity in business. This inevitably involved cutting themselves loose from the convention that all women were nurturers whose identity was sublimated in caring for their husbands and children. When younger women come into the office and talk about their children, reiterating their connection with a non-business world of dependence and submission, older women can see this as regressive, a back road towards the return of the old repression of ambitious women. For them, children were the enemies of promise; now motherhood is unprofessional.

Ambivalence

All this generational jockeying will end, no doubt, in a compromise establishing a blueprint which accepts motherhood as an integral part of the working way of life. This may involve employers' provision for childcare, government tax concessions, or a shift in men's attitudes demanding more participation for themselves in family life. But women, too, have to sort out their own ambivalence and confusion on this issue. Anne's experience gives some idea how complex this process is:

'There I was, over thirty, divorced, no kids, and all the old things about mothering instincts. Domestically it went into the cats – now I'm really a mother, they don't get a look-in. A mixture of mothering instincts and child instincts went into mothering my boss at work. I think for me, too, I'd been working twenty years and it had got dull. Having a baby wasn't necessarily going to destroy my relationship with my employers. My fear at twenty-five would have been that having a child was the end of my life. I had no sense of myself then. Anyway, there I was, life beginning to look a bit dull. I had a house and car, I could pay my bills, but nothing much seemed to be happening. I couldn't make a change at work, and I decided that I did want a radical change and that one day I would be very sad if I hadn't had a child. I didn't want the intensity of just work.

'I have a relationship with a man who is much younger than me, and he assumed he would have children. I decided that unless I was prepared and able to have children, I would have to let him go. I could do other things. Having a child was a hurdle to get over, like facing something I'd put aside for the last twenty years – the fear that a child was going to trap me and ruin my life. There was a lot of fear about this, but at one particular moment the fear of not ever having a child was greater. But it was like using a child to change my life.'

Anne was thirty-nine when she had her baby:

'My brain went. I couldn't believe anyone would ever take me seriously again. Bits of my brain are still coming back, eighteen months later. My vocabulary went down – I could count the words I used on my fingers. It was primitive and I couldn't recall certain words. I still practise on a cross-word to grasp language again – which is really about grasping ideas again.

'I had been warned by a lot of women. A friend of mine had a baby very recently and I spent a couple of days with her. She was the most boring person on earth, no conver-sation, glued to the baby. You're tired, just locked into the world of this baby.

'Having the baby stunned me. I felt awful resentment. I felt I'd made a terrible mistake. Everything was wrong. What you have with a baby is something that makes demands on you twenty-four hours a day and you can't escape, and that was the most frightening thing. It didn't matter how much responsibility I'd taken at work. It was impossible to think about work – I was getting worried if I could even work again. I hadn't even thought how I was going to manage.'

Lisa is younger than Anne – not yet thirty. She has a little girl of eighteen months:

'I think I'd always expected I would have both a career and a family. From the start, even when I was pregnant, I never really came to terms in my mind with the fact that the two things are incompatible. To a certain extent they are. I always wanted both, and thought I'd have both. I didn't put off having children in career terms, but because I didn't personally want to give up as much as you have to give up when you have a child. I knew what it would involve. I'd seen other people have children. I always loved and wanted them, but I'd got to be prepared to give something up. I am, anyway. Working part-time, I find my ambition has been tempered. The way I describe my career at the moment is it's on hold. I haven't gone backwards because the company has been really good. What I'm doing isn't a menial job, but it's not progressing my career, it's keeping it where it was. I'm quite happy about that at the moment. But other people will have gone on ahead and I can't catch up, and how long can I allow that? I don't know, but probably not more than the five years I envisage. And even then there'll be people I was way ahead of that are now ahead of me. But I think you have to accept that. It doesn't worry me now, but it would have done before. For example, there were three of us on very equal terms – group heads – and while I was on maternity leave, one became deputy managing director. If I'd been there that would have really bothered me because I'd have wanted the job, but it didn't bother me at all. It was a man who got the job, but I'd have felt the same if it had been a woman. I don't compete differently. What makes more difference is if people have children or not. People who have children are more sympathetic on the whole, men as well as women.

'There was a lot of angst about having a child. In one part of my mind I thought I was prepared to make the personal sacrifices. And I thought I loved my job. I didn't even try to reconcile them. Even when I was trying to get pregnant, I didn't know what I was going to do. It does change your attitude. The child becomes the most important thing – your influence and your life. It's not so for all women – some go back to the old routine. But I didn't want someone else to bring up my child. I know a woman in advertising who went back full-time when her baby was three months old. I find I do slightly disapprove of mothers like her putting themselves so much first. It's another person. You have to compromise. I really love my job and the company, and I wasn't sure I could give it up. I thought I wanted to be with the baby, though I know people who've said that and been crawling up the walls after six months. But I find it hard to imagine not doing my job. I was very lucky to be offered part-time.

'Even so, I resent it that men compromise much less. My husband's life has changed relatively little. It came as a surprise to me that he carries on so much as if nothing has happened. He'll work late without thinking about it. Even on the days I work, I can't stay on for a drink in the pub because I have to come home to the nanny. If I ask him to come home, he will if he can, but it doesn't come naturally. I resent it that he doesn't offer more.'

Weighting the Scales

Here is the nub of the problem for many successful and ambitious women who have children and want to continue their careers. I described earlier how their marriages or partnerships are based on an assumption of equality, but having a baby changes this balance between the parents. Several women expressed considerable resentment that the result of a decision taken jointly to become parents should affect the mother fundamentally, but make little impression on the father's routine. Anne finds it difficult to adjust to her partner's attitude to the relationship as it is now changed by the baby:

'I hadn't realised that I'd still feel the old thing that he should provide for all of us. He's a different generation from me, much younger, and both his parents worked and he doesn't understand. His expectation of women is what I think a man's expectation should be, but I'm not quite that woman.

'I didn't think the creative, motivated side of me would survive after the baby. I'd decided before I had the baby that I'd have to continue working – not just for income, but because it was the only thing that would keep me sane. But my biggest complaint – and I hear it from other women – is that my life has changed immeasurably and the father's hasn't been touched. He rings in the late afternoon and says do I mind, he's going to have a drink. A working couple think they have a relationship of some equality. They are well matched. But once the baby comes, that question goes out the window. She's part-time or her job goes, and they discover that they thought they had an egalitarian set-up but it's not. You suddenly see your partner in a different light. I see him as irresponsible, but his irresponsibilities mirror mine. Young women can go back to work on the same basis as their husbands, but in fact they have to bear the full burden of the fact that things have changed between them.

'Many women carry on as if they don't have a child. I don't envy it. I have a friend, Julie, who went back full-time and works 8 a.m. to 7 p.m. every day. I don't feel sympathetic to her working full-time. It seems to me I don't like the businesslike way such women go about having children. It's incredibly selfish – having a child to suit them in their relationship because she has reached a point in her career where she can negotiate a return to work. She was pregnant, had labour, three months' breast-feeding, and that was motherhood. They just carry on with their lives. I don't understand the lack of emotion in all that. I'm surprised at my own strength of feeling about it. I suppose I don't feel you should have a child as though it was nothing; it's a major thing. You have total responsi-bility for someone's life and the less involved you are, the less you know and understand what's going on with them. I wonder if I do feel I'm giving too much to the child. She's very dominant in my life, even when I'm working. I don't think I've got the balance right, and why do I feel so strongly about those other women? It's almost as though I don't think they should be able to get away with it like that. It seems wrong to me to have a child and pay someone else, almost like a kind of luxury living. I'm not sure if I feel if I can't why should they. I have my child two days a week and I wouldn't want to swap them, but I don't want her more days than I have. If I just saw her at weekends when my partner's around, I can't believe I'd have the same relationship with her. Possibly I'm frightened by that group of women ten years younger than I am. Maybe these mothers who work full-time represent that generation for me. Both men and women have a good sense of what they want, and I'm unnerved by their coolness and the calculated way . . . perhaps they're more in control of the world. I dislike their lack of muddle. I feel we should have muddle because there's so much conflict all the time. Their apparent sure-footedness makes me insecure.

'My sister-in-law never had any doubt about work – and it's something she has pursued at the cost of her daughter's interests. What's awful is that I'm excluding my brother from this separation – in a way I assume he can go on as before. My feelings are very ambivalent.'

It is inevitable that motherhood should cause such a personal conflict for ambitious career women. Many genuinely feel they are having the best of both worlds. This is certainly easier to achieve, though, when the gender balance of their relationship with husband or lover applies also to parenthood. Men, as we have seen in the business system, *are* questioning traditional masculinity and rediscovering female aspects of their nature. One day parenthood could become gender-balanced.

No, No Regrets

In the meantime, a number of successful younger women are demonstrating that womanhood today embraces both career fulfilment and motherhood. Lisa insists that motherhood enhances her professional performance:

'I was eager to get back. I missed it a lot – the people and the commercial side, seeing things work.

'I find I do work differently – more to do with being part-time than anything else, perhaps. But being a mother gives me an added purpose, a future to work for. I waste a lot less time. I get through what I used to do in three and a half or four days in two days. You get through so much, you realise how much time you waste, but that's also part of the job. I worry that I'm missing the social side, the team part. I miss out on not chatting.

'People's attitudes change, too. People value what you

say more because they can't have access to you most of the time. I haven't felt discounted because I'm a mother. Where I have noticed it particularly is with clients when they ring you at home. I tell them they can ring me at home and you can tell, when clients or colleagues without children call, that they half expect you to be a gibbering idiot, because you are now with a child and your mind must have turned to jelly. In the office you may be all right, but when you're with the child, clearly your brain's gone. I could tell they didn't expect a sensible answer, and were surprised when they got one.

'I have someone who works with me, and I worried that he might feel he'd got a part-time person telling him what to do, and it might be a problem. It actually worked out well – I've told him it's a real opportunity for him that I am part-time, because he can show his talents.

'As to the effect on me – I'm more relaxed, and life has slowed down 50 per cent with the child. I have more time to myself. I'm nowhere near as stressed. There's always pressure, which I enjoyed, but I enjoy the slower pace of life. It makes me wonder if I'll ever go back to working 8 a.m. to 8 p.m.'

Bond or Bondage?

And Anne, whose flow of work as a freelance has been hit by the recession, is now looking for a part-time job 'doing anything, just to earn some money'. Without a career to pursue, she says, she feels she is a less effective and stimulating mother. While friends who have returned to work full-time after their babies tell her they long for someone to talk to casually about anything but work, she misses the stimulus of the social side of work:

191

'I think the reason young-mum relationships are not as satisfying as work relationships is that they're monotonous and single-subject. There's something very helpful about having women around in the same position as you, but what you then talk about is your similar position, and that can get quite dull. You actually have conversations about nappies. I find the way I break out is to become rather unpleasantly curious about how they're coping with their partners.

'Our mothers didn't even find out the sort of world they were living in, let alone prepare us for the world we'd be in. I see a danger that I'll repeat the mistakes by over-protecting my child. I've become a governor of a little local school and they have a word processor for the three-to-four-year-olds. I have a kind of repugnance for technology, yet work will force me to keep abreast of my child's life. I find since I had her I don't take part in commercial daily life in the same way. I'm much more locally centred. A qualitative change has taken place in my work. It has made me go back into my intellectual abilities rather than my observant abilities. I rather welcome that. It's much tougher.

'What I think my child needs to see in me is someone who's working, so my staying at home isn't to give her an example, but to give her the confidence and stability in the home to enable her to make confident choices about what she does later.'

Elizabeth Cady Stanton, quoted earlier in this book, said in 1848: 'When assertion no longer seems dangerous, the concept of relationships changes from a bond of continuing dependence to a dynamic of interdependence. Then the notion of care expands from the paralysing injunction not to hurt others to an injunction to act responsively toward self and others, and thus to sustain connection.'

It is important for career women to 'sustain connection' with all areas of their lives. This is what makes their management style and their working morality different from men's. That connection involves children. If many successful women feel that children and ambition do not mix, maybe that is because the business culture has not yet shifted radically enough from the masculine blueprint. This could be the last corporate male bastion to fall, because a business system which would include motherhood as an integral aspect of high-powered women's success is still difficult for many women to accept. It has taken them too long to win the battle against societal pressure that motherhood is their major function in life. But as the business culture embraces women's priorities, it will happen.

Friendship

Relationships with men and children develop for many women within the context of longstanding friendships. Most very successful women refer to their 'girlfriends' with gratitude and a kind of relief. Between women friends, there is no pretence. When an ambitious career woman is operating on the limits of what she believes is acceptable 'female' behaviour, there is great comfort and security to be gained from knowing that another woman knows this and loves you regardless.

Sarah sees herself as a completely different person from the eighteen-year-old who applied for a job as a management trainee away from her home town because she kept bumping into her jilted fiancé:

'Being successful in business has changed my personality. I'm different in my social life as well because I've got so used to making decisions and saying what I think. I don't think it makes you that easy to be with. I always know what I want. I'm very close to my middle brother and he laughs. I'm hopeless at prevaricating now – I used to do it with bosses. I have different friends, and fewer of them. Definitely with boyfriends. It would be very difficult for me to be married. I have a live-in housekeeper, but on the social front friends get thinner on the ground.

'I still have girlfriends and old friends. I just don't fit into a niche. I'm not that easy on small talk and going to cocktail parties. There are times when you want someone to be there for you. My women friends can't be. They're great as emotional props and support, and they know what you mean, but when you're talking about stress and pressure of business they don't understand what it's like. I'd like to meet someone who said "There, there". My parents played that role, and when they died I felt very lonely. They were always on my side.

'I have two good girlfriends. Both have told me I've changed. One likes me better, one doesn't. One is very proud, so what I do is all right with her. I found she'd collected all the cuttings about me in her bedroom. The other rather wishes it was her. She was very bright and gave up to marry and have babies. She makes little digs.'

Several successful businesswomen confessed to being lonely because their long-term relationships with other women change as their lives and interests diverge. After the break-up of her first marriage, Janet found it tough being mother, father and breadwinner to three children while business was going badly. She found it very painful to feel herself alone on one side of a gulf between her experience and her interpretation of women's role that separated her from other women:

'It was terrible to be looked upon by other women in the way I was. Not so much at work, but when I left the children at school and couldn't stay to chat to the others. I was considered an oddity. They thought it weird I should work. They had hang-ups because the nanny collected my kids. I never made any friends in many years living in a smart London suburb until that crop decided they should have jobs. I minded that they cut me out. It's terrible not to have female friends you can talk to. I was probably seen as a very isolated person, and I was.'

When Andrea's business seemed in danger of collapse in its early stages, she found her women friends eager to welcome her back into the fold of non-working women:

'Women friends were very important to me. They were brought up like me, and we understood each other. Now some think I'm an admirable freak. But a lot of the energy which now goes into my business was invested in friendship. I've changed, and women friends are not as important to me now as they were.'

As more women take their careers for granted, and infiltrate further into the upper echelons of management, their friendships with other women will change. All women know the value of their female friendships, often forged for life at school or college. Such friendships, though, are strongest when one or other woman is in trouble or distressed. They flourish on mutual support and understanding – an equality of need. Success for one and not the other can actually undermine the balance of the relationship. This is not to say that women friends are necessarily bonded by failure, or that one friend cannot wholeheartedly rejoice at the success of another – as long as she is confident on some level of her friend's continuing need for her. The need for support or comfort is a basis for the mutual equality of friendship. Sarah, for example, mentioned that her women friends can no longer understand her problems because they have no experience of what her work involves. Sheila goes back to the mining village where she grew up and says she picks up with her friends as though they had never been apart. But she does not talk about her work, or where she's been. Those friendships still work because she gives the impression of being the same person as she was when she left to study astrophysics at university. She still needs something from her old school friends, and she knows what it is: 'We just spend the time talking about all the laughs we had. We share a lot of laughs.'

7

WOMANHOOD
REINVENTED

THE growing numbers of ambitious and successful women in business all have one thing in common: they are females out to invent themselves. As Simone de Beauvoir said, 'One is not born, rather one is made, a woman'. Once a woman accepts that, she can make what she will of her identity. Today's successful women are not the first to do so, but the numbers now involved make this personal self-invention a continuing and public process, because as each forges her own identity, she does not define just her own relationship with society. She is shaping future stereotypes for acceptable roles for all women.

Public Persona versus Private Person

A successful woman has a problem of compromise between her public persona and her private self. Public perception may not be critical of her business self, but it is unlikely to match her view of her inner self. *En route* to success, most women feel they have compromised natural behaviour to deal with circumstances where they feel a 'performance' would be more effective. So Sally, whose first ambition was to be an actress, says she has found that talent very useful in her management career: 'It meant that when I was lacking confidence, I could still put myself across as though I was naturally assertive.'

School head Karen says:

'I find when I have to confront people, which I don't like doing, that I suppress my natural inclination all the time. I have engineered a scene with a male subordinate where I was very angry about something he did, and sat down and planned losing my temper with him. But when my natural inclination is to blast off at people, which it usually is, then I keep that in and use a soft approach along the lines "Let's see if we can sort this out together." It's always we, not you, so I take a share in the blame. I must admit I often feel more like slapping a face, but one thing I have learned as a manager is to be much more tolerant of other people's feelings.'

Training director Ellen, chief executive Sarah, personnel director Suzanne and recruitment company director Valerie have all said they found themselves cursing and swearing – utterly out of character – as a way of gaining acceptance among male colleagues. Suzanne says:

'I think it makes men feel safer, as though you're not such an alien creature. There's also the point that if you don't they can feel constrained to temper their own behaviour and be awkward with women there. I don't want to keep underlining my difference from them. My whole intention is to show I'm no different, just very good at my job.

'I do remember, though, that someone told me once that one of the guys had said to her that I'd got a pretty face, but when I opened my mouth, all this ugly talk came out. Men can be very peculiar about it, anyway. There was one union meeting where one bloke called for a motion of censure on the managing director because he'd said fuck to some of the blokes in the all-male print shop. I said, "What's a few fucks between friends?", and the men were disgraced. I think what happens is they won't let you in unless you're one of the boys, but once you are one of the boys, they're afraid you're fundamentally better than they are. They think as long as you're ladylike, you can go back to being a mere woman at any moment. Silly sods.'

Male Reactions

Incidentally, if what Suzanne says suggests that successful women instinctively use the Trojan Horse approach to the male-dominated system, it should perhaps be said that once they have infiltrated it they can expect no bloodless coup. Many men hate this new breed of successful business colleague more than they have ever hated the most extreme man-hating feminist. Not only do such men – and there are many of them – view ambitious women as trying to take what is rightfully theirs, but they also see these women moving the goalposts and playing the business game by rules which penalise masculine strengths like competitiveness, aggression, ruthlessness. It is usually inadequate men who respond like this, but that is not the point. Their reaction ranges from resentment at 'preferential treatment' given to women to a real thirst for vengeance. There seems to have been a spate of murders over the last two years which are tragic examples of the way this hatred can become twisted. We have seen several individual killings where men have targeted ambitious young career women, and at least two of the most notorious mass killings in North America in recent years have involved inadequate men with a grudge against aspiring women.

Generally, men's perception of women at work is still the one which gets public airing. Management decisions are often based on male assumptions about the kind of work women are best at – that is, unless and until women change those examples within the system. The 'caring' personnel and public-relations fields can be in danger of being set aside as female ghettoes, while more 'intellectually robust' areas like finance remain a male-only province. It is greatly to women's credit that they have resisted what is an attempt to marginalise the skills they have excelled at. But by insisting on maintaining high and absolute standards of professionalism, women have ensured that fields where they are strongly represented remain central to the corporate agenda. Julie says:

'I hope channelling is beginning to break down because it didn't have the effect some senior management wanted. They had hoped to have a kind of two-tier board, where areas like personnel and training, where there are women directors and senior managers, would not be given as much priority as finance or research and development. It is true personnel and marketing have a higher proportion of women than others, and that's partly because women want to work there. They are not so often attracted to operations or finance. They prefer the people areas rather than those associated with more male-type skills. You can't generalise, but that's part of it. Education plays a part, too. We were recruiting graduates last year for jobs in finance. Usually we get equal numbers of male and female applicants, but this time there were very few women, and we asked why.

The jobs required particular finance qualifications, and the women didn't have them. They had different, but not the appropriate, ones.'

Similarly, for a long time all women in the House of Commons were steered into women's specialities, women's issues. Only since Margaret Thatcher brought the concept of housekeeping into the Treasury have either Labour or the Tories appointed women to senior positions there. Both Labour MP Harriet Harman and Conservative MP Edwina Currie are confined to areas of interest where ambitious men can say 'Oh, we've got a woman looking after that for Them', and feel that is all that needs to be done. Gillian Shephard says:

'In areas of ethical concern, I think the public is more likely to trust a woman. By the same token it's interesting to see that with our two Ministers in the Department of Social Security, it was agreed that Michael Jack rather than Ann Widdicombe would be responsible for single parents, where one might expect Ann would be assigned to it automatically as a woman.'

Established institutions – particularly those involved with funding, like banks – also tend to have a blanket prejudice against women who try to break away from old conventions. This must be cultural, since it involves male and female managers alike. In effect women who have been given enough rope to start up businesses based on their skills – which necessarily tend to be home- and care-orientated – are often denied help which would allow them to grow up and expand businesswise. This came up in Gillian Shephard's breakfast briefing meetings:

'The women tended to divide into those who said banks are just businesses who go into a deal, and those who said they can't take the banks on. Each said the banks don't have confidence in me as a woman, or as a black woman, and I have difficulty here. All found the banks very sticky when they want to expand. That next stage is when they have problems.

'I think expansion is difficult for women – moving into loans and taking on staff. That's where I think you need to put encouragement, effort, and training. I think women have a greater problem, and it's the step where most people need help. It's a move away from the maternal thing, my baby/my business, and it's difficult to let anyone else in. It's a fear of losing control. And yes, I do think banks smell nervousness. It was the very confident women who had no problems with them.'

Julie, as the senior woman director in her company, is responsible for equal opportunities. She argues that a highly placed man converted to the cause of ambitious women is more effective in bringing about equal opportunities than she and her female colleagues are:

'Now we have a new, more open management structure, and a chief executive who is committed to equality, management involvement in the issues is much stronger. My job could be done by a man, and I can see advantages in that. My female predecessor and I were strong on it and people thought nothing of it, because as women we would be, wouldn't we? But when a male director argues our case, he's not thought of as just mouthing off, and coming from a man, he has more clout, I'm sorry to say.'

There are signs of change. For instance, Ms Annabel Hands, who set up Britain's first professional female plumbing firm, won the 1990 Small Business of the Year award. One reason for her success, she said, is that many male clients liked the fact that she is a woman because they did not have to admit being unable to sort out their problems for themselves in front of a man. At one time they would have died rather than let a woman see their humiliation.

Public Perceptions

Thanks to the ignorance of the media, particularly newspapers, unsophisticated public perception of what qualifies success in business and management still tends to include 'masculine' as a vital ingredient. Science has measured the genetic difference between male and female as 4 per cent of DNA, but the public still expects to judge a successful woman in business by the degree of masculinity she exhibits. Karen describes parents' reaction to her appointment as school head:

'There was a problem being female with parents. The men tried to intimidate me, and came to my office to do it . . . My office is close to the school entrance, and one day I heard a woman saying she wanted to see the head. I came out and asked if I could help. She said she wanted to see the head. I said, "I'm the head". And she said, "You're a bit young, aren't you?" I just said no, how could I help, but I was so cross. She'd never have said that to a man, even if he only looked fifteen. She wouldn't have dared. There are people – men and women – who can't take a woman seriously in what they think is a serious position of responsibility.'

But even public opinion is more sophisticated about management and business than it was. More workers than ever before own shares in their companies, more people at all levels of society have become involved in mortages and interest rates and private pensions, and these developments have increased general understanding of how business works and interacts with society as a whole.

Because of the 'new' industries like technology, communications and information, which have no entrenched track record of male dominance, people are also gradually getting used to seeing professionalism without reference to sex. Lisa thinks that comparatively new industries free of habits of gender bias have helped by interacting successfully with traditional corporate hierarchies:

'I've found no prejudice against women in advertising in terms of promotion within the company. We do come across a few clients who wouldn't be happy with a woman or a black. They're not all men, either. There's a woman client who gives my agency's female account director such a hard time, and the agency won't give in. I wonder if for her sake they should, because she's never going to get anywhere with this client.

'I've found that the more straight and traditional the company, the more they expect that all agency people are weird – men with pony tails, and women! I've been involved in an advertising campaign for a bank. I know from people there that if I worked for the bank, they'd ignore me, but because I'm an outsider they listen because they think agency people are strange anyway.'

The Laggards of Europe

Many women – as well as men and the media – do still reject the process of change in business. Some feminists see self-interest as the main ingredient of feminine ambition, and feel that successful women betray the cause of the female sex.

Rather than colonise the male system, women should replace it with a female one – essentially its opposite. Some women take the view that if business cannot be fitted into a female-dominant mould, then business is 'immoral'.

But this is not what the successful women within the present system want, whether they feel themselves victims of male discrimination and chauvinism or not. What they want is to colonise business – and success and ambition – and create a democratic gender-balanced system worked by people, where men and women equally can invent their own professional identity.

A gender-balanced corporate system is still some way off. When I call the women I talked to change-agents, we have to remember that they are a minute percentage of working women. Within the system – particularly outside the international city centres – corporate convention still often sees the highly motivated and ambitious career woman as weird or strange, or committed to her career to compensate for something missing in her formative relationships with men.

This point is underlined by the reaction of many very eminent women recorded in the transcript of questions and answers after Dr Christine de Panafieu's speech to the Royal Society of Arts where she described British women as 'the laggards of Europe'. Dr de Panafieu, you may remember, argued that throughout the EC women are a gathering force for social change. In Britain, though, her research showed that progress is threatened by too many disaffected or apathetic women, and a lack of the necessary 'change-agent' female types. The accepted critical mass to bring about change is upwards of 30 per cent. The UK could show only 16 per cent.

Most of the British women who heard her speech in the audience at the Royal Society of Arts were outraged. Their response was to cast doubt on Dr de Panafieu's research. They accused her of not knowing what she was talking about in the 'special case' of British women. Very few seemed to be prepared to discuss the significance of what she said, or what they, as successful women in their own right, might do to help correct the balance between the laggards and the forward thrusters.

It is against this quasi-patriotic intellectual drag that any group of ambitious and successful women have to force their way forward. Dr de Panafieu's research quantified a national characteristic most successful women in business recognise only too well. Lesley lives and runs her own business in the North-West, but her experience can be matched anywhere in the country:

'My husband died, and I was left with two children aged ten and twelve. I had worked part-time as a computer operator for a large firm, but that didn't bring in enough money to support the family, and I wanted to be at home for the children. My husband was killed in a car crash, and it was a great shock to all of us. The children were very disturbed and insecure afterwards.

'I didn't have much money to put into equipment or anything like that. So I set myself up as a freelance, producing manuscripts and reports mostly for self-employed business people. At least I was at home, and if it meant I did a lot of work in the evenings after they'd gone to bed, it suited me to have something I had to do because that's when I missed my husband most.

'I had very good friends, and sometimes I had to work rather than have them round to talk or whatever. It was all right at first, but gradually I found it made them very angry that I was beginning to make it on my own. When I got someone in part-time to help out because there was so much work, they turned quite nasty. Who did I think I was? What made me different? Most of them were single parents, and they didn't see why I couldn't go on welfare like the rest of them.'

The British Welfare State Mentality was not invented with the welfare state. King Arthur and the Knights of the Round Table may be the first mythic evidence of its existence, but throughout history it has shaped the system of power. From feudalism, the relationship between people and monarchy, to the Church of England as guardian of law and order – all divided society into the powerful with a responsibility to provide, and those who could only hope (or claim the right) to be looked after. What I am trying to say is that we have a long-established tradition in our society which recognises that most people sometimes, and some people most of the time, need support. The political balance between the haves and the have-nots may ebb and flow, the comparative numbers in either group may change, but this division in society remains. It seems to me that when a variety of factors – recession, unemployment, ill-health, high levels of homelessness, and many more – place a large number of people in need of society's support, there can be a backlash against the 'strong' who are self-sufficient. This is reflected, I think, in the public perception of successful women in business.

The successful women themselves cannot afford to be sanguine. They like what they do, and more and more, as their numbers increase, so that they can feel themselves part of a powerful drive for change, they like what they are. But they pay a price. As they establish a business persona, some are uncertain about their own identity on a personal level. Karen says:

'An awful lot of female heads are single, and I think the reason why is that the degree of dedication doesn't leave time. Eventually you get so you've no other topic of conversation but the job. And a school is such an enclosed world.

'Relationships with people arise out of work and you tend to forget you don't have a personal relationship involvement. You can find yourself talking to them in a way perhaps you shouldn't – it's not professional. Professionality is a very big issue. The old-style head was part of the community, so it's hard to distance yourself. As far as they're concerned, you're theirs, owned by the community. That's got to change through good management, but it's going to be tough until the public at large see running a school as a management job and the head as a manager rather than a particular type of person.'

It is going to be tough for all change-agent women until the public at large – and other women in particular – welcome ambition and success as an accepted part of womanhood. The real test of their achievement will lie in the potential their example will unleash in other women in the workforce and at home. Their formula for womanhood could empower all women to make choices on their own account about their future role. That would be a prelude to a real gender balance, and a new definition for the business culture – humane.

SELECT REFERENCES

p. 6   Stephan and Woolridge, 'Sex Differences in Attributes for Task Performance', published by *Sex Roles Journal* 1977

p. 8   Hansard Society report, *Women at the Top*, published by the Society in January 1990

p. 13   Robert Bly, *Iron John: A Book About Men*, published by Element Books September 1991

p. 33   Deborah Tannen, *You Just Don't Understand: Women and Men in Conversation*, published by Virago 1991

p. 35   Lenore Harmon, *Journal of Counselling Psychology* 1970

p. 35   Elizabeth Cady Stanton speaking to reporters after the 1848 Seneca Falls Conference on Women's Rights, which adopted A Declaration of Sentiments modelled on the Declaration of Independence.

p. 41   Douglas LaBier, *Modern Madness: The Emotional Fallout of Success*, published by Addison Wesley 1986

p. 51   Carol Gilligan, *In a Different Voice*, published by Harvard University Press 1982

p. 62   Marina Horner, 'Toward an Understanding of Achievement-related Conflicts in Women', *Journal of Social Issues* 1972

p. 88   Marsha Jacobsen and Others, 'Women as Authority Figures' *Journal of Social Psychology* 1977

p. 115   Laura Tracy, *The Secret Between Us: Competition Among Women*, published by Little, Brown & Co. 1991

p. 149   Professor Ellis Cashmore quoted in *The Sunday Times*, 11 November 1990